Institution of Law Enforcement and Constitutional Developments - Emerging Trends and Enduring Debates

Edited by John R. Hermann and Paul Oluwatosin Bello

Published in London, United Kingdom

Institution of Law Enforcement and Constitutional Developments - Emerging Trends and Enduring Debates
http://dx.doi.org/10.5772/intechopen.1009055
Edited by John R. Hermann and Paul Oluwatosin Bello

Contributors
Adewale A. Olutola, Caia Marcee, Ibrahim Bangura, Jacek Wojnicki, Jarosław Szymanek, John R. Hermann, Nicolás Jorge Negri, Paul Oluwatosin Bello, Tamar Hopkins

First published in London, United Kingdom, 2026 by IntechOpen
IntechOpen is the global imprint of INTECHOPEN LIMITED, registered in England and Wales, registration number: 11086078, 167-169 Great Portland Street, London, W1W 5PF, United Kingdom

For EU product safety concerns: IN TECH d.o.o., Prolaz Marije Krucifikse Kozulić 3, 51000 Rijeka, Croatia, info@intechopen.com or visit our website at intechopen.com.

British Library Cataloguing-in-Publication Data
A catalogue record for this book is available from the British Library

Institution of Law Enforcement and Constitutional Developments - Emerging Trends and Enduring Debates
Edited by John R. Hermann and Paul Oluwatosin Bello
p. cm.
Print ISBN 978-1-83769-897-4
Online ISBN 978-1-83769-896-7
eBook (PDF) ISBN 978-1-83769-898-1

Meet the editors

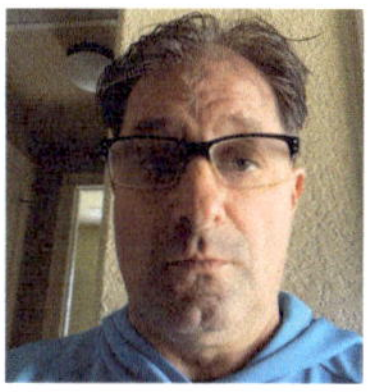

Dr. John R. Hermann is a tenured professor in the Department of Political Science at Trinity University in Texas. He has published twenty-five peer-reviewed papers. His research focuses on protecting vulnerable and marginalized groups in our constitutional republic and on higher education pedagogy, with particular attention to changing demographics in the United States.

Dr. Paul Oluwatosin Bello is a research associate and lecturer at the Independent Education Institute (IIEMSA) in Emeris, Ruimsig, South Africa, previously known as Monash South Africa. He obtained his doctorate in policing from Tshwane University of Technology in Pretoria, South Africa. Over the past decade, Dr. Bello has been actively involved in a wide range of research in policing and criminology, focusing specifically on the intersections of the criminal justice system, human trafficking, and social policy. He has authored more than fifty (50) peer-reviewed research publications addressing various criminal justice issues, including responses to human trafficking, police use of force, procedural justice policing, police legitimacy, offenders' perceptions of correctional officers, and the legitimacy of correctional officers. Dr. Bello has presented papers at both local and international conferences and has supervised four (4) Ph.D. students as well as several other postgraduate students to successful completion. Additionally, he serves as an external examiner for multiple universities, having examined over six (6) Ph.D. theses and twelve (12) master's dissertations. He is also a member of the Criminological Society of Africa.

Contents

Preface

The book *Institution of Law Enforcement and Constitutional Developments - Emerging Trends and Enduring Debates* explores two distinct but interrelated topics – Constitutional Law and Law Enforcement (those who enforce constitutional and other statutory schemes). While the book's overarching structure is interrelated, the editors have decided to divide it into three distinct sections. The book begins with Section I: *The Introduction*. The editors, John R. Hermann and Paul Oluwatosin Bello, co-write the Introductory Chapter titled "Constitutional Law and Law Enforcement: Emerging Trends and Perennial Debates." The central purpose of the chapter is to introduce the audience to the key concepts of constitutional law and law enforcement, enabling them to understand the nuances of their respective subjects.

The second section of the book is *Constitutional Law*. It starts with an empirical analysis of redistricting by the Supreme Court of the United States in John R. Hermann and Caia Marcee's "Judicial Review, Redistricting, and Politicalization of the Court". By contrast, Nicholas Jorge Negri offers a more normative discussion in "The Constitution as a Political Program and Legal System: An Integral Analysis in Service of the Common Good of Individuals". Jaroslaw Syzmanek tackles the vital topic of constitutional philosophy in "Evolutionary Interpretation in Constitutional Law: Between Accommodation and Instrumentalization". Constitutional Law concludes with Jacek Wojnicki's "Perspective Chapter: New Tendencies in Post-Communist Constitutionalism – The Case of Central and Eastern Europe".

The third section of the book covers the salient issue of Law Enforcement. Paul Oluwatosin Bello and Adewale A. Olutola empirically examine police misconduct in Africa, "The Crisis of Confidence: Understanding the Effect of Police Corruption, Abuse and Brutality on Public Perceptions of Law Enforcement in Africa". Tamar Hopkins' "The Psychological Impact of Unjustified Police Suspicion" explores how our impressions of the police affect our behavior. The section concludes with law enforcement issues in Guinea in Ibrahim Bangura's "The State, the Police, and Instability in Guinea: Reflections on Institutions of Security in a West African State."

In conclusion, the editors are supremely fortunate to work with Ms. Tea Jelaca, our publishing process manager. Ms. Jelaca kept us on task and offered guidance when we needed clarity. The book would not exist without her steady hand.

Equal editors:

John Hermann
Department of Political Science,
Trinity University,
San Antonio, United States of America

Dr. Paul Bello
Faculty of Humanities,
Independent Education Institute (IIEMSA), Emeris,
Ruimsig, South Africa

Section 1

The Introduction

Chapter 1

Introductory Chapter: Constitutional Accountability and Institutions of Law Enforcement – Emerging Trends and Enduring Debates

John R. Hermann and Paul Oluwatosin Bello

1. Introduction

The "Introductory chapter: Constitutional accountability and institutions of law enforcement: Emerging trends and enduring debates" offers a survey of the important issues involving the subject matter. This chapter is divided into two broad subsections: constitutional law and institutions of law enforcement.

1.1 Constitutional law: Introduction

This chapter discusses the fundamental elements of a successful United States Constitution. It also explains how powers that are sacred to Congress and the courts are now under the president's purview. There is much precedent for the president seizing powers from the other branches of government, especially during times of crisis.

1.2 The fundamentals of the United States Constitution

Creating a government structure, delineating the processes, and enumerating the powers and limitations of government are the minimal requirements for virtually any constitution [1, 3]. The United States Constitution, the longest-living one, meets these minimal requirements. It also embodies four central concepts: separation of powers/checks and balances, supremacy clause, federalism, and civil rights and liberties. Separation of powers involves the parceling out of certain tasks to each branch of government. The legislature has the power of the purse, the president has the power of the sword, and the judiciary has the power to interpret the law. Checks and balances refer to the system whereby one branch has oversight of another branch (e.g., the veto). The Supremacy Clause ensures that the Constitution and federal government are supreme to state interests – unless it is a power reserved to the states (e.g., family). Federalism is the allocation and balance of power between the federal government and the states. Certain powers belong to the federal

IntechOpen

government (e.g., war, coining money), others belong to the states (e.g., family and education), and some powers are concurrent (e.g., taxing, spending, and setting up a republican form of government). Finally, civil rights focus on the government actively protecting equal opportunity (e.g., 14th Amendment Equal Protection Clause), while civil liberties guarantee rights that are free from government interference (e.g., Bill of Rights and the 14th Amendment Due Process Clause). It is also vital that the people consent to be governed and that the process for selecting leaders is perceived as fair and just [1, pp. 3–10].

Another central feature of our constitutional system is that the framers opted for the Whig (i.e., the legislature is naturally the strongest branch of government) over the Hamiltonian (i.e., the legislature and executive are equal in power) model for federal government power [2, p. 16]. This is why Article I, Section 8 of the United States Constitution contains the most powers for Congress in comparison to the two other branches [2]. However, with the President Donald J. Trump administration, it is shattering constitutional norms and consolidating power, making the executive branch potentially the strongest. The Trump administration has eliminated many of the checks that belonged to the Senate (i.e., firing independent agency actors without Senate oversight), has decreased the importance of the bureaucratic state (e.g., eliminated thousands of jobs from the 14 departments), placed military actors in urban Democratic areas (e.g., Washington, DC, Los Angeles), banned policies that were for greater civil rights (e.g., DEI), attacked universities and media [3], made Congress a substandard branch of government, and disregarded lower federal court rulings. One of the most interesting questions is where these presidential powers are derived from.

1.3 Precedent for an energetic and expansive president

There is historical precedent for the president seizing more powers at the expense of Congress, the courts, and the states. The seizure of presidential power is usually called de facto, extraconstitutional, or prerogative power [4]. It usually happens in times of crisis rather than in times of peace. Yet, when peaceful times return, the president does not return the powers to their rightful owner. The Civil War is a classic example. President Abraham Lincoln created a naval blockade without the consent of Congress. The power of war resides with Congress in Article I, Section 8. The Supreme Court reaffirmed these powers (and even expanded them) in *The Prize Cases* (1863) by declaring that war is present when the president perceives there is war.

While the Civil War expanded presidential power, the Great Depression is when presidential power reached new heights. Starting in 1929, the president created the Office of Management and Budget, whereby the president played a coordinated and strategic role in creating the federal budget each year with Congress. Additionally, President Franklin Delano Roosevelt (FDR) created a large bureaucratic state that enforced the Office's policies (e.g., Public Works, Social Security). Finally, President Roosevelt created the legislative agenda, cementing New Deal policies that focused on social welfare over laissez-faire economics. Today, bills are often named after the president who introduced them. For example, the USA's health care plan is called Obama Care. Finally, in *United States v. Curtiss-Wright* (1935), the Supreme Court of the United States ruled that the president's powers in foreign affairs are plenary [5].

1.4 Expansive powers for President Trump

Based on subsequent events, such as 9/11, it is not surprising that the USA would eventually test the parameters of executive power. While President Trump had guardrails during his first term (both structural and personnel), these checks and balances are going by the wayside during Trump's second term. Having an undivided government gives the Trump administration maximum power to implement his policies. Questions of due process rights, protection of LGBTQIA + rights, and diversity programs are no longer to be part of public life (Diploma Divide). President Trump is not only changing the structure, processes, and limitations on government; he is defining the cultural war. He is also filling up election positions with election deniers from 2020.

1.5 Conclusion

The question that remains for President Trump is whether he can accomplish his goals of securing power before the midterm election in 2026. If President Trump were to have a divided government in either house of Congress after the midterm elections in November 2026, the changes he made to the constitutional order and the changing of norms may not be durable. After all, we are a country that broke away from the King of England for fear of a strong monarch. Americans are generally afraid of giving the president a blank check [+]. Since President Trump used executive orders to concentrate power, it may suffer from durability if an opposing party takes control of the White House.

This leaves the important question of the other subject matter of this edited volume: law enforcement.

2. Institutions of law enforcement

The relationship between law enforcement institutions and constitutional accountability represents one of the most critical intersections in modern democratic governance. Across cultures and jurisdictions, law enforcement institutions function as an important machinery of the state, tasked with maintaining public order, upholding the law, and protecting citizens from crime. The police, as the principal law enforcement institution in constitutional democracies, wield enormous powers in enforcing compliance. However, in discharging their constitutional duties, police officers often abuse their powers by acting arbitrarily, contravening legal boundaries, infringing on people's fundamental rights, creating tensions, and undermining the rule of law and democratic ethos. Such misconduct often pits them against citizens and can influence perceptions of the police and, by extension, the state. These instances of misconduct are both horizontal and vertical within the institution and are exacerbated by workforce crises, retention challenges, and financial strains, among other factors. These problems are clear indicators that a balance is needed between effective law enforcement and constitutional supremacy.

In recent decades, misconduct and other unethical practices recorded during police operations have generated concerns about why police officers deviate from the fundamentals of professional policing. These issues are even more explicit in this era of rapid adoption of artificial intelligence (AI) and the advancement of transnational organized crime. These concerns continue to remain a burning issue on the agendas of policymakers in many jurisdictions. Although reforms and other policy frameworks have been introduced to address this problem, the principal law enforcement institution remains entangled in these imbroglios.

The relationship between the public and law enforcement officials in many jurisdictions has remained marred by suspicion and distrust, fueled by the former's direct and indirect experiences with the police. Such distrust is also driven by police autonomy and asymmetric power relations between the police and the public, in which citizens are obligated to obey police orders even when they disagree, leading to pseudo-compliance. These experiences have brought police autonomy and prosecutorial discretion, which are integral to orthodox policing models and often insulated from judicial oversight, under intensified constitutional scrutiny. This engenders the necessity for police operational reporting, including tools that assess risk using algorithms, which have sparked debates about balancing law enforcement within the ambit of the law. These proposals mirror both modernization and durable standardization debates over the appropriate balance between security and liberation.

These challenges demand vibrant institutions that view law enforcement as an integrated system rather than a fragmented endeavor. Policymakers and other relevant stakeholders must prioritise long-term interventions over short-term reactive fixes. Such interventions must be proactive, rigorous, and periodically evaluated to monitor progress or success.

Author details

John R. Hermann[1*] and Paul Oluwatosin Bello[2]

1 Trinity University, San Antonio, USA

2 Faculty of Humanities, Independent Institute of Education, Emeris, South Africa

*Address all correspondence to: jhermann@trinity.edu

References

[1] Epstein L, Walker TG. Constitutional Law for a Changing America: Institutional Powers and Constraints. Eighth ed. Washington, D. C: Congressional Quarterly Press; 2014

[2] Reeves AJCR. No Blank Check: The Origins and Consequences of Public Antipathy Towards Presidential Power. United Kingdom: Cambridge University Press; 2022

[3] Grossman M, Hopkins DA. Polarized by Degrees: How the Diploma Divide and the Culture War Transformed American Politics. United Kingdom: Cambridge University Press; 2024

[4] Levitsky S, Zibatt D. How Democracies Die. New York, NY: Penguin Random House; 2018

[5] United States v. Curtiss Wright, U.S. 1935;**304**

Section 2

Constitutional Law

Chapter 2

Judicial Review, Redistricting, and the Politicization of the Court

John R. Hermann and Caia Marcee

Abstract

Redistricting exerts significant influence over political power by deciding who rises to prominence and authority. Through the manipulation of electoral maps in a process known as gerrymandering, individuals can limit the voting power of minority populations and allow candidates to prevail who otherwise may not. Additionally, scholarship lacks consensus on the negative or positive influences of redistricting (e.g., Gelman and King; Lain), requiring a deeper understanding of its interactions with the Supreme Court of the United States (SCOTUS). To that end, this study has two objectives: first, to determine how individuals fare in redistricting cases before SCOTUS during the 1963–2023 October terms; and second, to understand which factors, such as partisanship or race as a major issue in the case, explain these results. To answer these questions, the study conducted a statistical analysis of 92 redistricting cases decided by SCOTUS. The study finds that the percentage of cases decided pro-state remains constant irrespective of the independent variables included. By contrast, the results show that characteristics such as differing political parties, urban/rural interests, political realignments, and race influence the success of individual litigants. Of particular note was the politicization of the Roberts Court and its hostility toward the plight of individual litigants.

Keywords: constitutional law, judicial behavior, SCOTUS, redistricting, judicial review

1. Introduction

The issue of redistricting – the process of drawing electoral boundaries after every decennial census – has long been considered controversial [1, 2] ([3], 205). Still, redistricting is of vital importance to our constitutional republic. This study asks two distinct yet interrelated questions: First, how do individuals fare in redistricting cases before the Supreme Court? Second, what factors contribute to the decisions of the Supreme Court regarding redistricting? The influence of five explanatory variables is estimated: a) the presence of a differing dominant political party of the Court from the dominant party of the litigating state; b) whether the case took place during the Reagan political (and secular) realignment; c) the presence of race/ethnicity as the major issue in the case; d) the presence of political party as the major issue; and e) whether the case concerns a population dispute between urban and rural districts. The core issue in the case may include more than one independent variable, such as both race and political party. While there are many different ways of examining Supreme Court decision-making (e.g., doctrinal constitutional analysis), this study used mixed methods with descriptive statistics and qualitative analysis. By using mixed methods, we have a more thorough approach to examining redistricting cases.

While redistricting has always been a salient issue, it has not always been a judicial one. Prior to 1962, litigants who lacked voting power in urban areas had to turn to the states or Congress to define their voting rights. Supreme Court of the United States (SCOTUS) remedied this in *Baker* v. *Carr* (1962) [4]. This decision meant that if a litigant filed a Fourteenth Amendment Equal Protection Clause violation, as opposed to an Article IV, Section IV republican form of government challenge, the Court is able to adjudicate and provide a judicial remedy [4]. Additionally, SCOTUS created a "one-man, one-vote" principle in *Reynolds* v. *Sims* (1964) and *Wesberry* v. *Sanders* (1964) under the Equal Protection Clause in the Fourteenth Amendment [5, 6]. Based on the precedent from the decisions in *Baker*, *Reynolds*, and *Wesberry*, SCOTUS determines when and why a redistricting plan is constitutional or unconstitutional.

There is an additional reason to examine redistricting and malapportionment cases: Due to its ability to dilute voting power and limit equal access to the democratic process, redistricting holds significant implications for political power and presents a unique intersection with SCOTUS' power of judicial review ([7], 532). The manipulation of electoral maps through gerrymandering creates a system where voters are not offered equal access to the democratic process ([7], 533). It "turns democracy on its head – rather than voters choosing their representatives, it allows representatives to choose their voters" ([2], 150). Through judicial review, the Court can strike down these unfair maps in favor of more equitable districts, thus protecting the democratic process. Since redistricting and gerrymandering create districts "where one person's vote counts only a fraction (and sometimes[...]a very small fraction)" compared to that of another person, the use of judicial review to evaluate electoral maps is an essential role for SCOTUS ([8], 116).

The study proceeds by analyzing the relevant literature concerning redistricting and generating testable hypotheses. The study then outlines the data collection process, delineating each step in the identification of redistricting cases. After conceptualizing and operationalizing the independent and dependent variables, the study details the methodology, explaining the descriptive and inferential statistics used. Next, the study describes the findings, mixing quantitative and qualitative methods (e.g., case patterns in different decades), placing special emphasis on the changing ideological makeup and politicization of SCOTUS during the Roberts Court era. Finally, the study offers a conclusion with guidance for studying redistricting in the future.

2. Literature review

The literature review analyzes the existing research on redistricting. Focus is given to the relative influence of independent variables on the dependent variable, that is, which case characteristics influence SCOTUS deciding in favor of the individual over the state in litigation. In particular, the analysis of the literature examines the influence of a state's political parties, the dominant political party of SCOTUS, the influence of realignment theory, and the involvement of partisanship, race/ethnicity, or the urban/rural divide as a major issue in the case.

There are many influential factors considered in cases regarding redistricting. The many theoretical approaches combine with varying desired outcomes to produce a litany of important considerations that can come into conflict in redistricting cases. This conflict emerges because there is no established redistricting process beyond Article 1, Section 2 of the Constitution, which simply requires a decennial census and reapportionment ([3], 205). The lack of constitutional guidelines makes the Supreme Court's decisions of vital importance, but this is not without its own issues. In various cases, the Court has made redistricting cases justiciable, eliminated unequal representation, allowed for required majority-minority districts, restricted racial gerrymandering, allowed for partisan gerrymandering, and stated that the electoral system does not need to provide proportionality ([3], 216) [4–6, 9–12]. These cases have established guidelines that must be followed, but the Court has not yet created a clear standard by which to judge the constitutionality of redistricting plans.

The main reason for the difficulties associated with SCOTUS decisions on redistricting is the analytical tools utilized by the Court. Adjudication of a redistricting claim requires more than a demonstration of an infringement on an individual right; instead, it necessitates a comprehensive theory on democratic institutions and the correct form of representation. This means that to resolve a redistricting claim is to "decide how to structure the election process" ([13], 507). The Court typically employs an individual-rights framework that conceptualizes the claim as a concrete and personal harm, but often, in gerrymander cases, no individual has directly been denied the right to vote ([13], 506). Instead, these cases concern the ability of an individual to vote for a winning candidate, which is not a concrete right given to citizens. In any election, there will be winners and losers, and in any electoral map, there will be Democrats in Republican districts and Republicans in Democrat districts ([13], 507). This does not mean that each voter within these districts suffers a direct harm or has been denied a constitutional right. The nature of redistricting cases results in gerrymandering claims requiring a decision on the structure of a democracy and a conception of how to distribute legislative power amongst voters, which the Court is often unable to do. This results in decisions that conceptualize gerrymandering claims in extremely narrow conditions, producing a body of law that lacks a manageable standard and emphasizes the influence of case characteristics ([13], 506).

The first independent variable examined is based on the attitudinal/partisan model of SCOTUS decision-making. The attitudinal model "holds that the Supreme Court decides disputes in light of the facts of the case vis-a-vis the ideological attitudes and values of the justices" ([14], 65). The arguments presented before SCOTUS by the petitioning and responding attorneys are well-founded in precedent, articulated well, rooted in societal interests, and claim a constitutional ramification ([14], 64). Since both arguments are effective and well thought out, justices depend on ideological proclivities activated by various case stimuli to reach a decision ([14], 65). Since the "Supreme Court sits atop the judicial hierarchy" and "legal factors such as text, intent, and precedent are typically ambiguous, justices are free to make decisions based on their personal policy preferences" ([15], 273). This is further shown by an analysis of the influence of stare decisis on the decisions of Supreme Court justices conducted by Segal and Spaeth. They found that while stare decisis considerations may continue to be relevant, they are not the main basis for justices' decisions ([15], 985). Rather, justices will make decisions to advance their political preferences, even if it goes against the established precedent for that issue ([15], 974). In an analysis of their results, Segal and Spaeth contend that these findings might be time-bound to the more political SCOTUS seen during the Warren, Burger, and Rehnquist Courts ([15], 986). The political nature of the Court has only continued to grow, likely demonstrating an increased relevance of the attitudinal model of justice decision-making.

As the degree of partisan polarization across US society has increased, so has the partisan polarization and the politicization of SCOTUS. In 2010, with the appointment of Elena Kagan, all the Republican-nominated justices on the Court were ideologically to the right of all the Democrat-nominated justices ([16], 301). This speaks to an increasingly divided Court that is becoming more susceptible to partisan sorting. As the political elites who work to groom and identify good candidates for the Supreme Court become subject to more and more affective polarization, there is "growing ideological consciousness among the selectors of Justices and the Justices themselves" ([16], 303). This increased sense of ideology and growing schism between justices based on political identity work to reinforce the contentions of the attitudinal model. The inescapable partisan nature of politics infiltrates the deliberations of the Court and pushes justices to utilize political considerations both in addition to and in place of legal facts [14, 15] ([16], 306). Furthermore, the nature of redistricting decisions has gotten increasingly complex. As the Court has become more politicized, the legal and theoretical framework utilized by the Court has gotten progressively more unfit to handle the "more complex decisions demanded of the Court today" ([13], 513).

Due to the attitudinal model, the polarization of the Court, and the increasingly complex nature of redistricting cases, political parties have influence over various aspects of redistricting cases, especially when one considers the tendencies associated with either party. Those who identify as Republicans have a greater tendency to prioritize the interests of rural areas, the powers of the states, and are largely against racial redistricting to create majority–minority districts. On the other hand, Democrats have a greater tendency to favor the interests of urban residents, prioritize the individual over the state, and be in favor of racial redistricting for majority-minority districts ([17], 108–110). Due to these partisan inclinations, a central aspect of redistricting cases remains the dominant political party of the states and SCOTUS ([18], 259; [14], 70; [3], 210). For our purposes, the study uses the dominant political party as a proxy for the attitudinal model.

The first aspect of partisan influence viewed by this study is the relationship between the majority party of the state and the majority party of SCOTUS. Existing research establishes that the Supreme Court is more likely to rule a state law unconstitutional if the dominant political party of the Court differs from the dominant party of the originating state ([18], 271). The political considerations of justices, as advanced under the attitudinal model, suggest that justices are more inclined to rule a map unconstitutional if it goes against the opposing party of SCOTUS. Gates' analysis of 670 state statutes and constitutional provisions declared unconstitutional by SCOTUS from 1837 to 1964 found that the most salient cases often originate from states whose "partisan character is different from the dominant majority on the Court" ([18], 270).

This is further demonstrated by SCOTUS's position as a part of the national political alliance. With the capability to provide legitimacy to the laws of Congress and create policy themselves, SCOTUS maintains an influential position in the politics of Washington, D.C. [19, 20]. This creates a dynamic in which there is hostility between states of the opposing political party, especially in cases with essential political outcomes, such as redistricting. From Gates's findings, as well as the attitudinal model, this study hypothesizes that if the political party of the originating state differs from the dominant political party of the Court, the case is more likely to be decided in favor of the individual. But if the political party of the state and the Court are the same, the study expects those cases to be more likely to be decided in favor of the state. For example, if the state of Illinois has a dominant democratic state legislature and their map is reviewed by a dominant Republican SCOTUS, it would be more likely to side with the individual to limit the advantages built into the redistricting plan.

The influence of political parties on SCOTUS decisions also concerns political realignments and major party shifts in American politics. A political realignment is defined as "basic and enduring changes in the relative electoral power of the parties [. . .that] often entails changes in composition of the parties and the issues that divide them" ([21], 153). Realignments can directly influence SCOTUS through their connection with the lawmaking majority and the political nature of judicial decision-making ([18], 262; [19], 580). These durable shifts in political power happen in critical elections, which raise the profile of certain issues that proceed to cleave the populace and establish a new era of government.

These critical elections are "short-lived transitional periods when the old alliance is disintegrating and the new one is struggling to take control of political institutions" ([19], 580). During these transitional periods, the Court becomes misaligned with the lawmaking majority. This creates an era in which the cases reaching the Court are highly salient to the public, yet the Court's majority party lags behind that of the lawmaking majority. Through an analysis of the New Deal era realignment, Gates concludes that states with an opposing partisan nature to that of the Court will have a higher percentage of cases before the Court. He finds that many of the cases regarding democratically aligned issues were struck down by the majority Republican Court, likely in an "attempt to block Democratic policies" ([18], 272). The Court is more likely to hear and strike down cases from states with opposing partisan alignments, especially when the case concerns the most salient issue of that realignment.

The realignment analyzed in this study is the shift of political power from Democrats to Republicans with the 1980 critical presidential election. Although the presence of a realignment during this era is generally accepted, scholars are in conflict over the nature of this realignment and its influence on the politics of the 1980s and 1990s ([22], 132; [21], 166; [23], 130, 150). During this period, the era of conservative Democrats in the South came to an end, candidates' platforms gained more differentiation, and shifts in political domination occurred throughout the country. However, there is no scholarly consensus on whether it was a true political realignment ([21], 166). The conflict arises from the secular nature of the realignment; rather than happening in one "critical election," the Reagan realignment began with the electoral success of Reagan and culminated in Republican control of Congress in 1994 ([22], 130). Furthermore, rather than a nationwide shift in partisanship, the Reagan realignment happened predominantly in the South. As the ideological homogeneity of the parties increased, the South shifted away from its identity as conservative and Democrat to become a Republican stronghold ([22], 128).

Based on the findings of Gates and the nature of the Reagan realignment, this study hypothesizes that SCOTUS decisions after the 1980 critical election will be more pro-state than before. This is due to a greater separation between the political party of SCOTUS and the political party of the lawmaking majority ([19], 580). The study compares the outcomes of cases decided by the Burger Court before the 1980 critical election with those decided after the 1980 election and before the end of the Burger Court. Furthermore, the study hypothesizes that the shift in decisions siding with the states will increase with the transition to Republican domination and the increased politicization of the Court, with this rightward movement and increased partisanship more evident in cases originating from the South because of the secular nature of the realignment ([24], 1987).

There are many forms of gerrymandering that can result in a biased electoral map favoring one population over another. The three main types considered in literature are political party, race, and urban-rural divides. Based on *Rucho* v. *Common Cause* (2019), partisan gerrymandering is no longer a justiciable issue under the Article III, Section II case or controversy requirements ([11, 3]; 203). Separate from partisan-based gerrymandering, much existing scholarship is dedicated to investigating the outcomes and interactions of "redrawing district lines to advantage one racial [or ethnic group] of voters over another" ([25], 510).

Initially used to prevent racial and ethnic minorities from holding electoral influence, racial redistricting is now used to ensure minority representation through the creation of majority-minority districts. These are districts in which 51% or more of the population is of a single minority, and while they are often considered central to ensuring minority representation, they are also a source of concern and controversy ([25], 510). Such considerations include wasting votes through the oversaturation of minority voters in a single district, the concentration of minority votes when it is not needed, and reducing the number of electorally successful minority candidates ([25], 513 and 524). Supporters of plurality–minority districts, rather than majority–minority districts, claim that "African Americans can win from constituencies that are less than 50% Black, therefore Black-majority districts are not necessary and may place an artificial ceiling on potential Black gains" ([25], 513). If this is the case, then creating majority–minority districts harms, rather than aids, minority populations searching for electoral success.

Additionally, the influence of racial and ethnic redistricting, coupled with the disproportionate amount of political power prescribed to electoral maps, highlights the importance of race in redistricting and its consideration before the Court. From this scholarship and the findings of the attitudinal model, this study hypothesizes that the involvement of race or ethnicity as a major issue in a case will alter its outcome, with the direction depending on the party that holds the majority in the Court. We theorize that during periods of democratic domination of the Court, it will decide more frequently in favor of the individual, and during periods of Republican domination of the Court, it will decide more cases in favor of the state.

The last significant type of gerrymandering practiced is manipulating districts to separate urban and rural voters along partisan lines. Historically, the urban-rural geographic divide has led to the creation of districts with vastly different population sizes, giving unequal voting powers to individuals depending on where they reside ([3], 205). In addition to these population differences, distinct voting tendencies are associated with urban and rural citizens, which legislators take into consideration when redistricting.

Rural voters often identifying as Republican, while urban voters identify as Democrat, is typically attributed to demographic factors such as education, income, and race, due to the clear differences in party platforms on related issues ([26], 1362). Differing from the general understanding of this divide, Gimpel et al. (2020) find that voting differences are maintained even when controlling for various other demographic factors, such as race, income, education level, and more ([26], 1362). Along the continuum between rural and urban communities, there is a difference in how people live, whether they prefer dense populations or spread-out communities – the issues they feel are most important, and whether they feel neglected by political elites ([27], 163). This difference causes the "place itself [to become] political" ([27], 163). As cities grow and populations become denser, the partisan identities of the citizens change, shifting the successful political party ([27], 163). These differences incentivize political leaders to further separate these distinct populations into districts that benefit the political party in charge. From the findings of the attitudinal model, the proclivities of the parties, and the differences in voting tendencies between urban and rural citizens, this study hypothesizes that the inclusion of the urban–rural divide as a major issue in the case will influence the outcome of the case, depending on which party – Democrat or Republican – is in the majority of the Court.

3. Methods

The 92 cases regarding redistricting and reapportionment decided by the SCOTUS between its 1963–2023 October terms were identified through the Washington University Supreme Court Database (before the transfer to Penn State). Redistricting cases are defined as those concerning reapportionment (other than plans governed by the Voting Rights Act), residency requirements (durational, plus discrimination against nonresidents), voting, the Voting Rights Act of 1965 (plus amendments), and due process (jurisdiction over non-resident litigants). The study included cases that have only the decision types of equally divided vote, judgment of the court (orally argued), and opinion of the Court (orally argued); and the case involved the following legal provisions: Constitution, Constitutional Amendment, Federal Statute, State or local law or regulation.

The dependent variable in the study is whether an individual was successful in a redistricting case before the Court. The study defines an individual litigant as the party challenging the constitutionality of the electoral map in question, with an acknowledgment that these parties can be a single litigant, a group of individual litigants, a collection of class action lawsuits, as well as state officials. The individual litigant title is utilized because these parties are attempting to represent the interests of individual voters in challenging existing electoral maps. The independent variables are the presence of a different dominant political party in a state than the dominant political party of the Court, the presence of a realigning election, whether the case originated from the South, whether the case concerned an urban versus rural population dispute, and whether the case concerned a racial or ethnic gerrymandering claim. When considering the dominant political party of SCOTUS and the litigating state, the study uses the dominant political parties of the state House and Senate majorities as well as the governorship as a proxy for the dominant political party of the state. The partisanship of the state legislature is used instead of federal representation because the state legislature has direct control over redistricting. This makes state partisanship a more legitimate measure of the partisan leanings that are likely to be present in the maps and more clearly showcases the influence of political parties in Court decisions. The dominant political party of individual justices on the Court is measured by the political party of the president who appointed them, with the aggregate of all nine justices defining the dominant political party of the Court. The reference data for this explanatory variable came from data compiled by Carl Klarner from Harvard Dataverse, which includes the partisan makeup of state legislatures from 1937–2011, and data from the National Council of State Legislatures from 2011–2023 [28, 29]. For SCOTUS, the study used the dominant political party with each natural court. For the operationalization of all independent and dependent variables included in the study, see **Table A1**.

The remaining explanatory variables were similarly conceptualized. A case's classification as a realigning election case was determined by whether the case occurred during the Reagan realignment. This study defined the Reagan realignment as occurring from 1980 to 1986. This timeline, also used by Dahl (1957), provides ample time after Reagan's election for the Supreme Court to shift dominant parties, with an estimate of a new justice being appointed every 22 months. The influence of Southern cases was also estimated due to the secular nature of the Reagan realignment and its associated influences in the South, with this study defining the Southern states as the 11 states that attempted to secede from the union ([24], 1987).

Once the general trends of redistricting cases were unearthed, the study opted to conduct a more granular analysis of the Court under each chief justice. The Courts included in this study are Warren, Rehnquist, Burger, and Roberts. The general treatment of redistricting cases is considered, and then the relative influence of the explanatory variables on the dependent variable is introduced. A comparison of the success rates of individuals is conducted among the four different chief justices, with temporal changes to pro-individual outcome rates analyzed along each independent variable.

4. Findings

4.1 Aggregate findings

In aggregate, the study revealed several patterns in SCOTUS decisions on the issue of redistricting between the 1963–2023 October Terms. As evidenced by **Table 1**, the majority of redistricting and reapportionment cases decided by SCOTUS were in favor of the individual: SCOTUS gave a pro-individual outcome 57% of the time and a pro-state outcome 38% of the time. There were only five split decisions, meaning the Court reversed and affirmed in part, so these cases were not influential toward the final analysis. Additionally, as indicated in **Table 2**, the percentage of cases decided in favor of the state remains constant across varying case characteristics. Regardless of the presence of a different political party at the state level than SCOTUS, race, and urban/rural major issues in cases, SCOTUS's pro-state decision rate hovered around 38%.

Table 2 demonstrates that the percentage of cases decided in favor of the individual varies depending on the factors in the case. In cases where the

	Proportion
Pro-individual	0.57 (52)
Split decision	0.05 (5)
Pro-state	0.38 (35)
(n) number of cases.	

Table 1.
The outcomes of redistricting cases decided during the 1963–2023 October terms.

	No race	Race	Same party	Split party	Different party	No urban/ rural	Urban/ rural
Pro-individual	0.62 (23)	0.53 (29)	0.49 (13)	0.58 (19)	0.63 (20)	0.53 (32)	0.63 (20)
Split decision	0.00 (0)	0.09 (5)	0.074 (2)	0.09 (3)	0.00 (0)	0.08 (5)	0.00 (0)
Pro-state	0.38 (14)	0.38 (21)	0.44 (12)	0.33 (11)	0.38 (12)	0.38 (23)	0.38 (12)
Total	1 (37)	1 (55)	1 (27)	1 (33)	1 (32)	1 (60)	1 (32)
(n) number of cases.							

Table 2.
The influence of race/ethnicity, partisanship, and the urban/rural issue on redistricting cases: 1963–2023 October terms.

dominant political party of the state differs from the dominant party of SCOTUS, **Table 2** reveals a positive influence on individual litigant success. The study observes a 5% increase in pro-individual decisions compared to split-party states and a 14% increase compared to states with the same dominant party. This means that in cases from states with a different dominant political party, SCOTUS will have a higher likelihood of a pro-individual outcome than those cases from states with the same dominant party. The impact of the dominant political party on the outcomes of the cases is consistent with the findings of Gates (1987) that "the Court was prone to invalidate state policies [...] whose partisan or ideological orientation was opposed to the dominant majority on the Court" ([18], 275). This pattern is further exemplified through a comparison between *Rogers* v. *Lodge* (1982) and *Whitcomb* v. *Chavis* (1971). Both of these cases concern racial discrimination through non-single-member districts that limit the voting power of minority citizens, with one main difference: *Rogers* originated from a state with a different dominant political party, and *Whitcomb* was from a state with the same dominant political party as SCOTUS. *Rogers* v. *Lodge* was decided in favor of the individual (the current system did discriminate against minority voters), and *Whitcomb* v. *Chavis* was decided in favor of the state (there was not enough demonstrated proof of dilution of minority votes) [30, 31]. This showcases that even cases with similar characteristics and issues will be decided differently, possibly as a result of the attitudinal method of decision-making and the dominant political party of the originating state. As advanced by Segal and Spaeth (1993), since parties have differing proclivities and justices tend to make decisions based on their political preferences, the dominant political parties of states are an influential factor in redistricting case outcomes.

Table 2 also reveals that, on aggregate, the presence of race/ethnicity as the major issue in the cases negatively influences the individual litigant winning over the state interest. The study shows a 9% decrease in pro-individual decisions when race/ethnicity is a major issue in the case compared to when race/ethnicity is not an issue. This reveals an inverse relationship: the presence of race/ethnicity as a consideration in the case decreases the percentage of pro-individual decisions, possibly due to SCOTUS's dominant political party. In 1973, SCOTUS shifted from dominant Democrat to dominant Republican, at the same time the number of redistricting cases concerning race/ethnicity increased ([32], 311). In light of the partisan shift, the inverse relationship found with race/ethnicity as an issue is not surprising; since Republicans historically hold more pro-state views regarding racial/ethnic redistricting and prefer to maintain county and district borders rather than create majority-minority districts, it follows that a dominant Republican SCOTUS would decide racial/ethnic redistricting cases majority pro-state ([17], 108–110). Furthermore, the inverse relationship resulting from the partisan shift aligns with the findings of Segal and Spaeth: "justices make decisions by considering the facts of the case in light of their ideological attitudes and values" ([14], 73). The influence of racial considerations can be shown through a continued examination of *Whitcomb* v. *Chavis* (1971). This case included a racial discrimination claim challenging the presence of multi-member districts [31]. SCOTUS decided that multi-member districts did not present an issue, thereby siding with the state. Comparatively, in *Chapman* v. *Meier* (1975), SCOTUS presents a preference for single-member districts and a disdain for multi-member districts, siding with the individual in the case [33]. The lack of a racial discrimination claim in the case may have pushed SCOTUS toward a pro-individual outcome.

Additionally, **Table 2** reveals that in cases involving urban vs. rural population disputes as the major issue, there is a positive influence on pro-individual outcomes. The study shows a 10% increase in individual litigant success when cases concern urban vs. rural population disputes: those cases with the issue have a pro-individual outcome 63% of the time, while those that do not include urban/rural disputes have pro-individual outcomes 53% of the time. This relationship is positive, with the presence of an urban/rural dispute increasing individual success rates, a pattern that is likely due to the timing of these cases.

Population-based disputes were more prevalent under the more liberal Warren Court, which historically protected individual rights, leading to a higher percentage of these cases having pro-individual outcomes ([32], 276). This impact of urban and rural issues is consistent with Segal and Spaeth's attitudinal model and the differences found between rural and urban populations ([14], 70; [26], 1363). By concentrating voters of opposing political parties into different geographic areas, gerrymandering creates a tendency for the Court to favor the interests of the party currently dominating the Court. This can translate to either favoring the issues of rural voters if SCOTUS is predominantly Republican or urban interests if SCOTUS is predominantly Democrat ([14], 70; [26], 1363). The resulting link between the liberal Warren Court and urban/rural redistricting cases is exemplified by landmark cases such as *Reynolds* v. *Sims* (1964) and *Wesberry* v. *Sanders* (1964). These two cases altered redistricting and reapportionment nationwide for both state and federal districts by imposing an equal population requirement. Concerning Alabama state legislative districts and Georgia congressional districts, respectively, these cases marked major victories for urban interests and were decided by the Warren Court ([32], 279).

4.2 Granular analysis

The macro findings necessitated a more granular view of redistricting decisions, as there may be variation in success rates for the individual litigant among the chief justices. As revealed by **Table 3**, the success rates of individuals before each chief justice vary, emphasizing that there are tendencies across time that are overshadowed when viewing the entire universe of cases. The historically more liberal Warren Court had pro-individual outcomes 82% of the time. In comparison, the following Burger Court was pro-individual 52% of the time, the Rehnquist Court had a surprising pro-individual outcome in 62% of cases, and the Roberts Court dropped down to 33% of cases having pro-individual outcomes. This continuous drop in pro-individual outcomes from the Warren to the Burger Court is reflective of several trends: the drop in urban/rural cases, the rise of race/ethnicity-based cases, the transition of SCOTUS from a dominant Democrat to a dominant Republican, and a realignment that altered the political landscape of the country. The drop in pro-individual outcomes also demonstrates the increased politicization of the Court and the shift toward a Roberts Court unsympathetic to the individual. The almost 30% difference between the outcomes of the Rehnquist and the Roberts Court, as well as the almost 20% difference between the Burger and Roberts Court, demonstrates a shift in SCOTUS decision-making as the ideological gap on the Court grows ([16], 306). As the conservative majority on the Court becomes increasingly conservative and falls more in line with the ideology of the executive branch, the Court becomes more hostile to the arguments of individuals, as demonstrated by the outcomes during the Roberts Court.

The only court that does not follow this trend is the Rehnquist Court, which has a higher pro-individual outcome rate than its predecessor, the Burger Court. This finding is anomalous to our expectations, possibly due to a misspecified model. The types of cases heard by the Rehnquist Court differ from those heard by the Burger Court and, thus, the potential ramifications of a secular realignment in the South may have altered the ratios in the Burger Court.

One of the most influential factors in SCOTUS decision-making regarding redistricting remains the dominant political party of the originating state of the case.

	Warren Court	**Burger Court**	**Rehnquist Court**	**Roberts Court**
Pro-individual	0.82 (14)	0.52 (16)	0.62 (16)	0.33 (6)
Split decision	0.00 (0)	0.03 (1)	0.00 (0)	0.22 (4)
Pro-state	0.18 (3)	0.45 (14)	0.38 (10)	0.44 (8)
Total	1 (17)	1 (21)	1 (26)	0.99 (18)

(n) number of cases.

Table 3.
The outcomes of redistricting cases under each chief justice between 1963 and 2023 October terms.

	Warren Court								
	No race	**Race**	**Same party**	**Split party**	**Different party**	**No urban/ rural**	**Urban/ rural**	**Not south**	**South**
Pro-individual	0.87 (13)	0.5 (1)	0.83 (10)	1 (1)	0.75 (3)	0.5 (1)	0.87 (13)	0.88 (7)	0.79 (7)
Split decision	0.00 (0)	0.00 (0)	0.00 (0)	0.00 (0)	0.00 (0)	0.00 (0)	0.00 (0)	0.00 (0)	0.00 (0)
Pro-state	0.13 (2)	0.5 (1)	0.17 (2)	0.00 (0)	0.25 (1)	0.5 (1)	0.13 (2)	0.13 (1)	0.22 (2)
Total	1 (15)	1 (2)	1 (12)	1 (1)	1 (4)	1 (2)	1 (15)	1 (8)	1 (9)

(n) number of cases.

Table 4.
The influence of race/ethnicity, partisanship, and the urban/rural issue on redistricting cases under the Warren Court: 1963–1969 October terms.

In 1973, SCOTUS underwent a change in the dominant party, transitioning from a dominant Democrat to a dominant Republican ([32], 316). This shift not only altered its tendencies regarding critical issues such as redistricting but also shifted its relationship with states. As seen in **Table 4**, the Warren Court, dominated by democratic appointees, decided cases mostly originating from states with the same dominant political party, of which 83% had pro-individual outcomes. While this is contrary to our expectations regarding cases of the same political party, it follows the overall trend of the Warren Court to be pro-individual, as well as following the proclivities associated with the democratic party ([17], 108–110).

In comparison, subsequent courts followed different trends. As shown in **Table 5**, the Burger Court heard a majority of cases from either split-party states or states with a different dominant political party. The outcomes for the split-party cases were roughly 50/50, with half of the cases decided in favor of the individual and the other half in favor of the state. For those cases originating from states with a different dominant political party, 69% were decided pro-individual. This follows the expectations of the attitudinal model and Dahl (1957) and Gates' (1987) findings: Since "the Supreme Court is inevitably part of the dominant national political alliance" and justices act with ideological and party considerations, the cases coming from their opposing party should be decided pro-individual to reduce the power of the opposing party ([19], 580; [18], 260; [14], 70).

As evidenced by **Table 6**, the Rehnquist Court heard no cases from states with the same dominant political party but did see a difference in the rate of pro-individual outcomes between the split-party states and the opposing dominant party states. The cases from split-party states were decided pro-individual 73% of the time, while those from a different political party were decided pro-individual 45% of the time. The lack of same-party cases could show an increased partisanship in SCOTUS, but the split-party and opposing-party outcomes are contrary to expectations. The influence of ideology is still present because split-party states have opposing party members in power, but the drop in pro-individual outcomes in opposing states indicates that other factors could be more influential than political party, such as the central issue of the case.

	Burger Court										
	No race	**Race**	**Same party**	**Split party**	**Different party**	**No urban/ rural**	**Urban/ rural**	**Not realignment**	**Realignment**	**Not south**	**South**
Pro-individual	0.38 (5)	0.61(11)	0.00 (0)	0.46 (5)	0.69 (11)	0.58 (11)	0.42 (5)	0.44 (8)	0.62 (8)	0.31 (4)	0.67 (12)
Split decision	0.00 (0)	0.06 (1)	0.00 (0)	0.09 (1)	0.00 (0)	0.05 (1)	0.00 (0)	0.00 (0)	0.07 (1)	0.00 (0)	0.05 (1)
Pro-state	0.62 (8)	0.33 (6)	1 (4)	0.46 (5)	0.31 (5)	0.37 (7)	0.58 (7)	0.56 (10)	0.31 (4)	0.69 (9)	0.28 (5)
Total	1 (13)	1 (18)	1 (4)	1 (11)	1 (16)	1 (19)	1 (12)	1 (18)	1 (13)	1 (13)	1 (18)

(n) number of cases.

Table 5.
The influence of race/ethnicity, partisanship, and the urban/rural issue on redistricting cases under the Burger Court: 1969–1986 October terms.

	Rehnquist Court								
	No race	**Race**	**Same party**	**Split party**	**Different party**	**No urban/ rural**	**Urban/ rural**	**Not south**	**South**
Pro-individual	0.75 (3)	0.59 (13)	0.00 (0)	0.73 (11)	0.45 (5)	0.61 (14)	0.67 (2)	0.67 (6)	0.59 (10)
Split decision	0.00 (0)	0.00 (0)	0.00 (0)	0.00 (0)	0.00 (0)	0.00 (0)	0.00 (0)	0.00 (0)	0.00 (0)
Pro-state	0.25 (1)	0.41 (9)	0.00 (0)	0.27 (4)	0.55 (6)	0.39 (9)	0.33 (1)	0.33 (3)	0.41 (7)
Total	1 (4)	1 (22)	0 (0)	1 (15)	1 (11)	1 (23)	1 (3)	1 (9)	1 (17)

(n) number of cases.

Table 6.
The influence of race/ethnicity, partisanship, and the urban/rural issue on redistricting cases under the Rehnquist Court: 1986–2005 October terms.

Lastly, as seen in **Table 7**, the Roberts Court heard only one case from an opposing party state, and the outcomes for both split-party and same-party states were majority pro-state. Those cases originating from states with split parties had 33% pro-individual outcomes, while those from opposing party states had 27% pro-individual outcomes. This follows the expectations of the attitudinal model and emphasizes the increased importance of partisanship under the Roberts Court. As justices continue to make decisions based on personal preferences, the more conservative majority on the Court will prioritize the interests and outcomes that support a more conservative agenda ([14], 70). Additionally, this severe drop in pro-individual decisions showcases how the dominant Republican Party has shifted rightward as time has passed. Increased polarization has meant that SCOTUS has seen a shift in the ideological tendencies of justices: "Republican appointees on the whole are [...] more conservative than in the past while democratic appointees as

	Roberts Court								
	No race	**Race**	**Same party**	**Split party**	**Different party**	**No urban/ rural**	**Urban/ rural**	**Not south**	**South**
Pro-individual	0.4 (2)	0.31 (4)	0.27 (3)	0.33 (2)	1 (1)	0.38 (6)	0.00 (0)	0.5 (1)	0.31 (5)
Split decision	0.00 (0)	0.31 (4)	0.18 (2)	0.33 (2)	0.00 (0)	0.25 (4)	0.00 (0)	0.00 (0)	0.25 (4)
Pro-state	0.6 (3)	0.38 (5)	0.55 (6)	0.33 (2)	0.00 (0)	0.38 (6)	1 (1)	0.5 (1)	0.44 (7)
Total	1 (5)	1 (13)	1 (11)	0.99 (6)	1 (1)	1 (16)	1 (1)	1 (2)	1 (16)

(n) number of cases.

Table 7.
The influence of race/ethnicity, partisanship, and the urban/rural issue on redistricting cases under the Roberts Court: 2005–2023 October terms.

a group have not changed appreciably" ([16], 305). The results of this ideological shift are an increasingly conservative Court, clearly reflected in the hostile decisions of the Roberts Court that favor state goals over individual interests.

An analysis of the urban vs. rural cases shows a drop in frequency as time passes. As **Table 4** demonstrates, the Warren Court heard 15 cases that included an urban/rural dispute and decided pro-individual in 87% of them. Not only does this tendency align with the pro-individual trends evident in the Warren Court, but it also follows the proclivities of the democratic party. Democrats tend to favor urban areas and urban interests, while Republicans often prioritize rural areas and their respective values and norms ([17], 108–110). Faced with electoral maps that largely favored rural areas, the Warren Court remedied the lack of voting power in urban centers ([14], 70; [17], 108–110; [32], 279).

The front-loading of these cases on the Warren Court accounts for its highly individual overall outcomes. Since the most pro-individual Court decided the majority of the urban/rural cases, it is not surprising that the overall trend of the cases would be pro-individual ([32], 279). As time passes, the study observes a decrease in the number of urban/rural cases decided by SCOTUS. The Burger Court heard 12 cases, with 42% resulting in pro-individual outcomes. The Rehnquist Court heard only three cases concerning urban/rural disputes, and the Roberts Court heard only one urban/rural case. The drop in the frequency of these cases reflects the evolution of the issue of redistricting; once *Reynolds* v. *Sims* and *Wesberry* v. *Sanders* established the "one person, one vote" standard and SCOTUS enforced that standard, there was little debate or wiggle room within the population requirements of districts [6].

The influence and prevalence of the race/ethnicity variable followed the opposite trend: as urban/rural disputes faded as a central issue, race/ethnicity disputes rose and grew in frequency. **Table 4** demonstrates that the Warren Court heard only two cases that considered a race/ethnicity dispute, emphasizing the centrality of population disputes as the central issue of this time. As seen in **Table 5**, the Burger Court saw a drastic increase in the number of cases concerning race/ethnicity heard by SCOTUS, likely the result of the Voting Rights Act of 1965 (VRA). The central aspect of the VRA's influence on redistricting was Section 2, which "prohibits any state or political sub-division from imposing a voting practice which 'results in the denial or abridgement of the right of any citizen of the United States to vote on account of race or color'" ([25], 519). Additionally, Section 5 of the VRA established the requirement of pre-clearance: this means that for those states with a history of discriminating against minority voters, any changes to electoral maps or voting practices must first be approved by the Attorney General or will be litigated by SCOTUS ([25], 519).

The Burger Court decided 61% of cases involving race disputes pro-individual; this is much higher than the pro-individual rates of non-race/ethnicity cases and is also likely due to the VRA of 1965 ([25], 519). The literature suggests that following the implementation of the VRA, those states subject to pre-clearance requirements began to have a better civil rights support score than prior to the VRA ([25], 519). Since SCOTUS is part of the national policy-making coalition and subject to the political shifts in Washington and the general public, these changes in representative actions will also impact SCOTUS decision-making. This will likely lead to higher pro-individual rates for race/ethnicity-based cases decided under the Burger Court ([19], 580).

Evidenced in **Table 6**, the importance of race/ethnicity factors continued to grow as time progressed, with the Rehnquist Court hearing 22 cases involving race/ethnicity claims, 59% of which had pro-individual outcomes. The slight decrease in pro-individual outcomes delivered by the Rehnquist Court showcases the continued rightward shift of the Court. This trend is further exemplified in **Table** 7, with the Roberts Court having heard 13 cases involving race/ethnicity disputes and deciding pro-individual in only 31% of them. This drop in pro-individual outcomes shows a hostility toward individuals that is also expressed in the overall decisions of the Roberts Court and further demonstrates a rightward slide by SCOTUS. Additionally, the reduced number of race and ethnicity claims heard by the Roberts Court demonstrates an antagonism to these identity-based redistricting claims. The political nature of the race/ethnicity cases, as well as the politicization of SCOTUS, combine to create a court that is exceedingly unsympathetic to individual rights claims in general, with a specific aversion toward those cases aimed at ensuring equal representation for racial and ethnic minorities. These findings are supported by the contentions of the attitudinal model, which asserts that the policy preferences of the justices are part of the consideration in delivering decisions. As the Court becomes dominated by Republicans and more conservative members, cases are decided more in favor of conservative values that protect state rights ([14], 70; [32], 311). Furthermore, the decision of SCOTUS in *Shelby County* v. *Holder*, which ruled Section 4 of the Voting Rights Act of 1965 unconstitutional, removed the requirement for preclearance and effectively nullified Section 5 of the VRA [34]. This meant that historically gerrymandered areas were no longer required to gain preclearance for electoral changes. This decision has had a lasting influence over the issue of redistricting before the Court, leading to a greater proportion of cases being decided pro-state and a drop in the number of race and ethnicity cases heard by the Court.

The final variables included in the study were the presence of a political realignment at the time of the case and whether the case emerged from the South. Over the time included in this study, one political realignment occurred with the election of President Reagan in 1980. With the election of Reagan in 1980, public opinion shifted to be more in favor of the Republican Party, and the control of the federal government transitioned from Democrat to Republican ([22], 130). This variable is only considered for the Burger Court because this was the Court present for the entirety of the defined realignment years. As seen in **Table 5**, those cases between 1980 and 1986 were decided more in favor of individuals (62%) than those occurring under the same court but before the realignment (44% pro-individual). This supports the hypothesis that as the federal government transitions into a new regime, the Court remains out of touch and sides with the individual over supporting the new regime ([19], 580).

Another important feature of the secular Reagan realignment is the South variable, which identifies whether the case emerged from a Southern state. As the number of Southern cases increased from the Warren Court to the Roberts Court, the effects of the secular realignment are demonstrated by the rates of pro-individual outcomes. As the region transitions from predominantly Democrat to predominantly Republican, the relationship between the states and SCOTUS shifts to favor the state. **Table 5** shows that the Burger Court heard 18 cases from the South, with 67% having pro-individual outcomes. This is followed by a drop in pro-individual outcomes handed down by the

Rehnquist Court, as shown in **Table 6**: out of 17 cases from the South, the Rehnquist Court handed down pro-individual decisions in 59%. Lastly, as seen in **Table 7**, the Roberts Court heard 16 cases from the South, with 31% receiving pro-individual decisions. The higher pro-individual decisions present in the Burger and Rehnquist Courts are likely due to the presence of Southern conservative Democrats as the main political coalition of the South ([22], 128; [14], 70). This shifts with the dissolution of the Southern conservative sect of the democratic party and the subsequent realignment of the South to align with the Republican Party and its respective policies.

5. Discussion

5.1 Overall findings

Redistricting is a foundational practice in our constitutional republic. Yet, little is known about its treatment before SCOTUS. This study reveals the influence of various factors on SCOTUS's decisions regarding redistricting, finding that central issues of the case, as well as the partisan character of the emerging state, influence the case's outcome. The study finds that the presence of a population-based urban versus rural dispute increases the likelihood of a pro-individual outcome, while the presence of a race- or ethnicity-based discrimination claim reduces the likelihood of a pro-individual outcome. Furthermore, this research finds that partisanship influences the outcomes delivered by the Court. For cases emerging from states with a differing dominant political party than that of SCOTUS, the rate of pro-individual outcomes increases compared to the rate of pro-individual outcomes in cases from states with the same dominant political party.

In addition to these overall trends, the study finds patterns in each era of the Court investigated. As time passed, SCOTUS transitioned from being dominated by Democrats to being dominated by Republicans, continuing to move rightward until the Roberts Court, which was very hostile to individual litigants (as opposed to the state position) in virtually all cases. This animus is reflective of an increasingly ideological and political Court that prefers the advancement of state interests over the protection of individual rights. Additionally, the decisions handed down by the Roberts Court showcase a Court divided by political identity, in which the affective polarization of political elites has spread to the justices ([16], 304). Of particular note were the unsympathetic positions taken by the Roberts Court on racial/ethnic gerrymandering claims and the Court's complete lack of cases originating from states with an opposing partisan identity. Furthermore, the influence of partisanship in decision-making is evident in all Court's aside from the Rehnquist Court, which has a higher pro-individual outcome rate than expected.

5.2 Theory

Since a state-gerrymandered district that dilutes the voting power of certain populations will likely elect a representative who otherwise would not have won that election, the Supreme Court offers the last opportunity for many litigants who have been locked out of the electoral process. The reliance of the newly elected official on the socially-engineered map makes them less likely to address the issue of gerrymandering ([7], 533). This entrenchment of Congressional representatives in gerrymandering then necessitates the involvement of SCOTUS to restore democratic ideals, raising the issue of the countermajoritarian dilemma. As an unelected branch of government able to undo the actions of elected officials, SCOTUS's power of judicial review can go against the desires of the majority and, therefore, democratic theory: "[W]hen the Supreme Court declares unconstitutional a legislative act or the action of an elective executive, it thwarts the will of the representatives of here and now; it exercises control, not on behalf of the prevailing majority, but against it" ([35], 16–17). Although the process of declaring maps unconstitutional can be anti-democratic (i.e., an unelected Court ruling the laws of popular branches unconstitutional), the policy outcomes from such decisions often serve to preserve and protect democracy within our constitutional republic.

This is no different with redistricting. Through gerrymandering, states are denying populations their right to an equally weighted vote and limiting their ability to elect the representative of their choice. When SCOTUS strikes down a redistricting statute as unconstitutional, the decision may serve to restore the very democratic values that SCOTUS is often accused of violating. Ely supports this notion, arguing that when elected branches are not working as intended, SCOTUS should actively participate in "unblocking stoppages to the democratic process" ([8], 115). He continues by portraying the "denial of the [right to] vote [as] the quintessential stoppage" necessitating SCOTUS intervention ([8], 116). Lain further advocates for this idea, asserting that SCOTUS can protect rights that Congress cannot. By enforcing the will of the majority as opposed to the will of those in power, the Court is open to the appeals of citizens whose voices are not heard in Congress. Lain claims, "[w]hen widespread attitudes change but the law does not, pressure builds to implement that change-to give force of law to the transformation of attitudes, values, and policy preferences occurring in larger society" ([2], 117).

The ways in which justices reach their decisions will also influence the outcomes of cases, especially regarding redistricting due to its partisan influences. The attitudinal model holds that the justices engage in post hoc decision-making to achieve their preferred policy outcome ([14], 70). Following this theory, the outcomes of cases depend on the partisanship of the Court and the partisanship of the state from which the case emerges ([18], 270). The Supreme Court is more likely to rule a state law unconstitutional if the dominant political party of the Court differs from the dominant party of the originating state, reaffirming the attitudinal model of judicial decision-making. According to the attitudinal model, the facts of a case will influence the likelihood of a pro-individual outcome based on the preferences associated with the political parties and the dominant political party of SCOTUS ([14], 70). For instance, a Court with dominant Democrats will make decisions that benefit both democratic states and voters in urban areas, due to the association between Democrats and urban voters. The opposite holds true for Republicans: A SCOTUS that is Republican-dominant will make decisions that benefit Republican states and rural voters ([17], 108–110).

Two major goals of gerrymandering are to increase the power of one political party or influence minority representation. Although this study did not observe many cases that included a direct partisan redistricting claim, partisanship holds significant influence in the practice of implementing redistricting plans. The recent decision in *Rucho* v. *Common Cause* (2019) to remove partisan gerrymandering as a justiciable issue under Article III, Section II case and controversy requirements will only increase the importance of political partisanship [11]. By making partisan gerrymandering a political question unable to be heard by the courts, SCOTUS has opened the door for more complete partisan gerrymandering to go unchecked by the courts. With redistricting left up to Congress and the states, SCOTUS has entrenched the practice of partisan redistricting, possibly allowing it to grow more blatant and extreme ([36], 1014). This raises an important question: What other forms of redistricting will be deemed political questions and thus become unable to be heard by SCOTUS?

The influence of various independent variables in the study casts doubt on whether it is prudent for certain cases to come before SCOTUS. For instance, a case concerning racial or ethnic discrimination claims might want to center around an issue other than racial discrimination when going before the Roberts Court, because of its hostility toward individuals in cases involving race or ethnicity disputes. The inverse relationship between racial discrimination claims and pro-individual outcomes identified above, coupled with the current conservative and increasingly political environment of SCOTUS, suggests that these sorts of cases would not be very successful. The Roberts Court has shown itself to be hostile toward individuals: a 33% success rate exists for individuals, especially in cases involving race and ethnic discrimination claims. The low pro-individual decision rates of the Roberts Court become even more striking when compared to the Warren Court, which had an 80% individual success rate, further demonstrating the influence of the conservative movement on the Court. By taking these cases to this Court, pro-state decisions are likely to create precedents that will harm future individual litigants seeking help with a manipulated partisan map. With this hostile and unsympathetic Court, minority voters who have less voting power will need to use other avenues to address their complaints and grievances.

This trend extends beyond the complaints of minority voters and is evidenced by the recent redistricting case regarding Louisiana's electoral map that was deferred until the next term: *Louisiana* v. *Callais* (2024) [37]. The plaintiffs in the case are Caucasian voters who claim that the current maps are a racial gerrymander limiting their vote. This is a continuation of another case in which African American voters had sued the original map and won, requiring the state to redraw and implement another majority-minority district into the electoral map [37]. While the racial claim of discrimination against majority groups is unprecedented, the Roberts Court's decision to defer until the next term shows an unwillingness to deliver a pro-individual outcome and further demonstrates the Roberts Court's hostility to individual interests. Furthermore, by delaying SCOTUS's decision, the Roberts Court is ensuring the challenged map stays in effect for midterm elections, removing voters' last avenue of redress for their grievances [37].

5.3 Academic disputes

The academic community's disputes over redistricting's negative and positive influence in a constitutional republic highlight the importance of understanding this complex issue. Some claim that the presence of gerrymandering creates a cycle of "incumbent self-dealing," defined as "efforts by existing officeholders to entrench themselves and their party, regardless of constituent sentiment" ([7], 516). Klarman maintains that the manipulation of gerrymandering reveals various types of entrenchment in which power is taken away from the voters; thus, redistricting damages the constitutional republic. Lain supports these claims, arguing that the "party that controls congressional redistricting can maximize its chance of electoral success" ([2], 150). Elected representatives are not fairly chosen by the people, which goes against democratic ideals and harms the function of our constitutional republic.

The opposing side holds that the presence of any redistricting is a positive force within government, no matter its manipulations, due to its ability to routinely create political renewal and redistribution of authority ([1], 554). Through a comparison between gerrymandered districts and a complete lack of districts, Gelman and King (1994) conclude, "[r]edistricting in state legislatures has substantially increased electoral responsiveness and kept it higher than it would be otherwise for about half of all elections in each state" ([1], 553). Although the process can be manipulated to benefit certain parties, redistricting is better for the responsiveness of elected representatives than if there were a complete lack of districts. Furthermore, since districts are redrawn every decade and "[t]he effects of any one redistricting are not permanent, . . . the decennial redistricting process repeatedly injects the political system with a healthy dose of increased responsiveness" ([1], 553). Gelman and King conclude that "[f]ar from being a scourge on the political system in need of major reforms, legislative redistricting has invigorated American representative democracy," providing another perspective with which to view and analyze redistricting ([1], 554). The combined influence of these factors (increased responsiveness, reduced bias, and continual political renewal) transforms redistricting into a positive force in government.

By emphasizing the importance of fair redistricting, the debate captures the significance of this study. While the presence of redistricting and reapportionment enhances the quality of representation compared to no redistricting, there are flaws in the current system, as captured in the arguments of Klarman and Lain. The partisan and racial manipulation of districts influences the power of individual votes and the ability of certain candidates to be elected. Even so, the argument of Gelman and King also holds true: there is a benefit to, and a need for, frequent redistricting. The influence of partisan considerations in the decisions of SCOTUS, as demonstrated throughout the findings of this study, reinforces the conclusions of Klarman and Lain. While SCOTUS does effectively oversee certain aspects of redistricting and gerrymandering, the partisan influence present in SCOTUS decisions, combined with recent decisions concerning the justiciability of types of redistricting, speaks to difficulties in SCOTUS redistricting oversight. These issues necessitate solutions that will curb the partisan influence in redistricting without the need for SCOTUS oversight.

5.4 Future research

The issue of redistricting before SCOTUS deserves further study since the stability of the pro-state decisions showcases trends that are not captured in this analysis. For the rate of pro-state decisions to remain so constant, there must be factors that push SCOTUS toward pro-state decisions that are not considered in this study, thereby emphasizing the need for future consideration regarding redistricting and SCOTUS. The factors investigated in this study yielded results about the tendency of the Court to deliver pro-individual decisions, while they had very little influence over the rate of pro-state outcomes. Understanding the tendency of

SCOTUS to deliver pro-state outcomes is just as important as understanding the factors that influence their decision to deliver pro-individual outcomes.

Appendix

Variable	Operationalization
Dependent: individual litigant success	Case was decided in favor of the individual litigants. = 1 Court affirms and reverses in part = 0.5 Otherwise = 0
Independent: dominant political party of the SCOTUS vs. state	Dominant political party of SCOTUS different from state = 1 Split party state = 0.5 Otherwise = 0
Independent: realigning election	Case during Reagan realignment = 1 Otherwise = 0
Independent: south	Case from a Southern state = 1 Otherwise = 0
Independent: race/ethnicity	Case considers race/ethnicity as a major issue = 1 Otherwise = 0
Independent: urban/rural	Case considers urban/rural as a major issue = 1 Otherwise = 0

Table A1.
Operationalization of variables.

Author details

John R. Hermann* and Caia Marcee
Trinity University, San Antonio, USA

*Address all correspondence to: jhermann@trinity.edu

References

[1] Gelman A, King G. Enhancing democracy through legislative redistricting. American Political Science Review. 1994;**88**(3):541

[2] Barrett Lain C. Upside-down Judicial Review. Georgetown Law Journal. 2012;**101**(1):113

[3] La Raja R. Redistricting: Reading between the lines. Annual Review of Political Science. 2009;**12**(1):203

[4] Baker v. Carr, 369 U.S. 186. 1962

[5] Reynolds v. Sims, 377 U.S. 533. 1964

[6] Wesberry v. Sanders, 376 U.S. 1. 1964

[7] Klarman M. Majoritarian Judicial Review: The Entrenchment Problem. Georgetown Law Journal. 1997;**85**(3):491

[8] Ely J. Democracy and Distrust: A Theory of Judicial Review. Cambridge, MA: Harvard University Press; 1980

[9] Thornburg v. Gingles, 478 U.S. 30. 1986

[10] Shaw v. Reno, 509 U.S. 630. 1993

[11] Rucho v. Common Cause, 588 U.S. 2019

[12] Davis v. Bandemer, 478 U.S. 109. 1986

[13] Gerken H. Lost in the Political Thicket: The Court, Election Law, and The Doctrinal Interregnum. University of Pennsylvania Law Review. 2004;**153**(1):503

[14] Segal J, Spaeth H. The Supreme Court and the Attitudinal Model. Cambridge, England: Cambridge University Press; 1993

[15] Segal J, Spaeth H. The influence of Stare Decisis on the votes of United States Supreme Court Justices. American Journal of Political Science. 1996;**40**(4):971

[16] Baum L, Devins N. Split Definitive: How Party Polarization Turned the Supreme Court into a Partisan Court. The Supreme Court Review. 2016;301

[17] Grossmann M, Hopkins D. Polarized by Degrees: How the Diploma Divide and the Culture War Transformed American Politics. Cambridge, England: Cambridge University Press; 2024

[18] Realignment GJP. Unconstitutional State Policies, and the U.S. Supreme Court. American Journal of Political Science. 1987;**31**(2):1837

[19] Dahl R. Decision-Making in a Democracy: The Supreme Court as a National Policy-Maker. Emory Law Journal. 2001;**50**(2):563

[20] Casper J. The Supreme Court and National Policy Making. The American Political Science Review. 1976;**70**(1):50

[21] Campbell J. Polarized: Making Sense of a Divided America. Princeton, New Jersey: Princeton University Press; 2016

[22] Abramowitz A, Saunders K. Ideological realignment in the U.S.

electorate. The Journal of Politics. 1998;**60**(3):634

[23] Rosenof T. Realignment: The Theory that Changed the Way We Think about American Politics. New York, NY: Rowman & Littlefield Publishers; 2003

[24] Black E, Black M. Politics and Society in the South. Cambridge, MA: Harvard University Press; 1987

[25] Canon D. Race and redistricting. Annual Review of Political Science. 2022;**25**(1):509

[26] Gimpel J, Lovin N, Moy B, Reeves A. The Urban–Rural Gulf in American Political Behavior. Political Behavior. 2020;**42**(4):1343

[27] Scala D, Johnson K. Political Polarization along the Rural-Urban continuum? The Geography of the Presidential Vote, 2000–2016. The Annals of the American Academy of Political and Social Science. 2017; **672**:162

[28] Klarner C. Data on State Legislature Partisanship. Harvard Dataverse. 2025

[29] National Council of State Legislatures. Available from: https://www.ncsl.org/about-state-legislatures/state-partisan-composition

[30] Rogers v. Lodge, 458 U.S. 613. 1982

[31] Whitcomb v. Chavis, 403 U.S. 124. 1971

[32] Schwartz B. A History of the Supreme Court. Oxford, England: Oxford University Press; 1995

[33] Chapman v. Meier, 420 U.S. 1. 1975

[34] Shelby County v. Holder, 570 U.S. 529. 2013

[35] Bickel A. The Least Dangerous Branch: The Supreme Court at the Bar of Politics. New Haven, CT: Yale University Press; 1962

[36] Williams N. Partisan Gerrymandering: The promise and limits of State Court Judicial Review. Marquette Law Review. 2023; **106**(4):949

[37] Louisiana v. Phillip Callais, et al., 24-109

Chapter 3

The Constitution as a Political Program and Legal System: An Integral Analysis in Service of the Common Good of Individuals

Nicolás Jorge Negri

Abstract

The Constitution, beyond being a mere compendium of norms, stands as the foundational act of a global political organization, outlining the fundamental rules that govern both the exercise of political power and social coexistence. Its nature is inherently dual, simultaneously encompassing a dimension of political program, which expresses the aspirations and purposes of the nation, and a dimension of legal system, which establishes the normative framework and institutional structure. The modern understanding of constitutional law underscores this integration, conceiving the discipline as a unity that interweaves political science and constitutional science, recognizing the inseparability between norms and political reality. This "new political and constitutional science" seeks to be the "law of reality," transcending mere dogmatic analysis.

Keywords: constitution, Argentina, common good, reality law, policy

1. Introduction

The Constitution, beyond being a mere compendium of norms, stands as the foundational act of a global political organization, outlining the fundamental rules that govern both the exercise of political power and social coexistence [1–5] ([6] Rosatti, 2025; [7]). Its nature is inherently dual, simultaneously encompassing a dimension of political program, which expresses the aspirations and purposes of the nation, and a dimension of legal system, which establishes the normative framework and institutional structure. The modern understanding of constitutional law underscores this integration, conceiving the discipline as a unity that interweaves political science and constitutional science, recognizing the inseparability between norms and political reality. This "new political and constitutional science" seeks to be the "law of reality," transcending mere dogmatic analysis [8]. At the core of this duality and its interconnection lies a supreme objective: the achievement of the common good and the safeguarding of human dignity and liberty. This fundamental purpose constitutes the "ideological ceiling" of the Constitution, guiding all its provisions and their practical application [7–9]. This report aims to analyze the Constitution from these two complementary perspectives, demonstrating their intrinsic link and their ultimate orientation toward the common good of individuals. It will examine how the political program establishes the vision and aims of the nation, while the legal system provides the structure and guarantees to materialize these purposes (**Table 1**).

Dimension	Description	Key sources	Associated concepts
Political program	Vision and purposes of the nation, aspirational aims, societal project: 'the why'.	Preamble, programmatic clauses (Art. 75, inc. 18, 19).	Common good, communitarian personalism, human dignity, liberty.
Legal system	Normative structure, rules of the game, organization of power, guarantee of rights, 'the how'.	Art. 31 (Supremacy), Arts. 14, 17, 18, 19 (Rights), separation of powers.	Constitutional supremacy, rigidity, rule of law, control mechanisms.

Table 1.
Political Program and Legal System.

2. The Constitution as a political program: Vision and purpose of the nation

2.1 Fundamental aims and objectives: The societal project

In most nations that have followed the American model (US, 1787), the Constitution transcends the mere function of a fundamental legal document to operate as an authentic "plan or program of government" and a "symbol of national unity." In this capacity, it expresses the sentiments, aspirations, and intrinsic values of a people, reflecting their idiosyncrasies and way of being [8]. The fundamental objectives of the nation are explicitly articulated in the Preamble of the Argentine Constitution. These include the following: "To constitute national unity, strengthen justice, consolidate internal peace, provide for the common defense, promote the general welfare, and secure the blessings of liberty." These purposes extend "to ourselves, to our posterity, and to all men in the world who wish to inhabit Argentine soil." The Preamble, therefore, is not just an introduction but the ideological foundation that gives meaning and direction to the entire constitutional text. It acts as a teleological compass, ensuring that every provision is interpreted and applied in service of these foundational aims. Any interpretation or legislative act that deviates from this spirit, even if formally correct, would lack substantive legitimacy.

In addition to the Preamble, the Constitution incorporates programmatic clauses that detail national aspirations. Article 75, paragraph 18, known as the "progress clause," is a clear example. Originally, this provision established a plan for the country's prosperity, promoting industry, immigration, and the development of infrastructure such as railways and navigable canals. The constitutional reform of 1994 broadened this vision through Article 75, paragraph 19, which now emphasizes "human development, economic progress with social justice, the productivity of the national economy, the generation of employment, and the professional training of workers" [1, 7, 9]. This evolution of the "progress clause" reveals a transformation in the conception of national welfare. Initially, the focus was predominantly material and economic, centered on productive growth.

However, the later inclusion of "human development" and "social justice" reflects a deeper recognition that progress is not measured solely in economic terms but in the quality of life and equity for all citizens. This change aligns with the emergence of the "social question" and the need for a "social rule of law" that would address the inequalities inherent in nineteenth-century individualistic liberal constitutionalism. Therefore, the Constitution adapts to reflect a more comprehensive and humanistic understanding of the common good, seeking development that benefits everyone and not just certain sectors.

2.2 The "ideological ceiling": Communitarian personalism

The predominant conception that informs the Argentine Constitution, its "ideological ceiling," is **communitarian personalism**. This perspective is distinguished by simultaneously affirming the intrinsic dignity of the human person and their inherent sociability. The Constitution does not conceive of the human being as an isolated entity but as an individual deeply interconnected with social groups and the political community. It recognizes a common good that goes beyond the mere protection of individual rights, seeking the fullness of the social group as a whole for the shared enjoyment of all its members [7, 9].

This ideological framework rejects both extreme individualism, which limits state functions to the protection of private interests, and totalitarianism, which subordinates the individual to the state or a collective entity [9]. The protection of human dignity and the limitation of public power, constitutionally enshrined, act as barriers against any authoritarian tendency [7].

Various constitutional provisions reflect this communitarian personalism. The Argentine Constitution is one such case. Article 19, for example, establishes a fundamental distinction between private actions, reserved for the individual's intimate sphere, and public or social actions that affect third parties or the social order. This clause protects privacy but also recognizes the social dimension of human conduct. Articles such as 14, 16, 17, 18, 28, 33, and 43, by declaring constitutional rights, place human dignity at the center of the political and legal system. These rights, preexisting state recognition and derived from human dignity, are not absolute and must be regulated to harmonize with other rights and the common good. The Constitution also recognizes rights for various social organizations, such as the family, trade unions, and political parties, reinforcing the personalist and communitarian perspective of society. Article 41, which enshrines the right to a healthy environment, introduces the notion of intergenerational solidarity by protecting this right for present and future generations. Article 75, paragraph 2, links the taxing power of Congress with the "public needs of the community" or the "general good of the State," extending this logic to the foundation of other governmental powers. Article 75, paragraph 23, mandates Congress to promote affirmative actions to guarantee real equality of opportunities, especially for vulnerable groups. Finally, Article 120 assigns to the Public Ministry the defense of the "general interests of society," aligning with the protection of collective goods [7, 9].

The identification of "communitarian personalism" as the "ideological ceiling" of the Constitution does not imply a static doctrine but a dynamic interpretive lens. When a Constitution incorporates various ideological components, the interpretation of its norms can be influenced by the "last imposed ideology" or by the "ideology of the operator." This generates a productive tension: While communitarian personalism establishes the predominant framework, its practical application and meaning evolve with society and its interpreters. The 1994 reform, by emphasizing social rights and affirmative actions, strengthened the communitarian aspect. However, interpretation by judges, legislators, and the executive ensures that communitarian personalism is not an immutable dogma but a living framework that is continuously redefined. The common good, in this context, is not a fixed concept but an objective in constant pursuit and re-prioritization through constitutional practice and interpretation, always seeking the balance between individual and collective flourishing. The common good, as a central concept in philosophy and political science, possesses essential characteristics that define it as the ultimate cause of the state, the sphere of state action, the foundation of public authority, and a synthetic legal value (**Table 2**).

Characteristic	Description
Foundational and necessary	It is the aim and constitutive principle of all political society, unavoidable for common life.
Ministerial and personalist	It is not an end in itself but a means to serve the human person and social groups, seeking their fulfillment.
Ethical	It seeks the improvement and perfection of society and its members, using means consistent with human dignity.
Cultural	It implies the active participation of humans in the construction of the political community, developing their vocation as co-creators.
Historical and dynamic	Its content, although containing permanent elements, varies across time and space, adapting to the challenges of each era.
Unitary and structural	It is not a sum of partial goods but an integrated structure where all aspects harmonize for the good of society.
Spontaneous and architectural	It is the fruit of social spontaneity and the foresightful direction of governors, requiring intelligence to organize cooperation.
Perfectible and gradual	It is never fully achieved; one can always aspire to better conditions of social life, gradually ascending.
Juridical and ideological	It implies a legal dimension, generating rights and obligations that, through distributive and legal justice, must be realized.
Problematic and conflictive	Human conflict and the scarcity of goods mean that its achievement requires agreement, dialog, and negotiation.
Subsidiary	It seeks to promote and complement the actions of individuals and smaller groups, avoiding excessive regulation and fostering creativity.
Real and concrete	It is not an abstraction but an existential reality that can be realized, enjoyed, and, to some extent, perceived and measured.

Table 2.
Characteristics of the Common Good.

2.3. Constitutional dynamics and adaptation

The Constitution is not a static document but a "living creation" that must adapt to the "changing needs of social life" [8, 9]. Its durability and effectiveness depend on its capacity to evolve without requiring constant amendments. This is achieved through drafting that favors "generality" and "flexibility," allowing the text to adapt to new conditions and requirements without losing its essence.

A concise and flexible Constitution is less prone to interpretive problems and the need for frequent reforms, which could compromise its stability.

In this adaptation process, constitutional interpretation plays a crucial role in maintaining the relevance and effectiveness of the text. **Dynamic or progressive interpretation** conceives of the law as a manifestation of human life in constant evolution, allowing its contents to adjust in a "reasonable and convenient" manner to the social needs of the present. This approach prevents reality from overflowing the legal norm, thereby preventing the system from becoming merely nominal and lacking practical validity. An illustrative example is the application of Articles 14 and 32, related to freedom of the press, to new media such as cinema, radio, television, and the Internet. The protection of free expression of thought, regardless of the medium, allowed these clauses to be extended to manifestations not foreseen in 1853/60, demonstrating how dynamic interpretation updates the Constitution without the need for formal reform [1, 2, 8].

Teleological or finalist interpretation is equally fundamental. This requires understanding the ultimate purpose of the Constitution, which is the "dominant political idea in society" [5, 8]. In a constitutional democracy, this purpose is centered on "limiting and controlling power in the safeguard of human liberty and dignity." All particular norms must be harmonized with this global purpose, rejecting any interpretation that disregards the major objectives established in the fundamental law.

Finally, **systematic interpretation** requires that all constitutional clauses be interpreted in harmony with each other, as the Constitution is an "organic whole" [9]. This method avoids attributing opposing meanings to provisions and seeks the coherence of the legal system [4]. Interpretation, in its various modalities (dynamic, teleological, systematic), acts as the essential bridge between the political program and the legal system. The political program establishes aspirational objectives, such as the common good, liberty, and justice. The legal system, for its part, provides the normative framework. Interpretation is the active mechanism that translates these abstract ideals into concrete legal applications, ensuring their continuous relevance in a changing reality. Without dynamic interpretation, the political program could become an "empty normative skeleton" [9]. Without a teleological focus on the common good and human dignity, interpretation could be reduced to a dogmatic exercise, detached from the fundamental purpose of the Constitution. This implies that the effectiveness of the Constitution in service of the common good resides not only in its original wording but in its constant and living interpretation by its "operators" (judges, legislators, executives) [9]. This interpretive function entails a continuous ethical responsibility to align actions with foundational values.

3. The Constitution as a legal system: Structure and guarantee of order

3.1 Normative nature and legal supremacy

The Constitution is defined as the fundamental legal document from which the validity of the entire legal system of a political society emanates. Its main normative function is to establish "guidelines for the organization and exercise of power" and "instructions on how social relations should be channeled" [8]. It is important to note that, although closely linked, the concept of "Constitution" as a document is not synonymous with "constitutional law" as a scientific discipline. Constitutional law encompasses the study of the Constitution but also extends to extra-constitutional political institutions and to political reality as a whole [4, 7].

A fundamental pillar of constitutionalism is the principle of the **supremacy of the Constitution**, which establishes it as the "supreme law" of the nation nación [1, 8, 9]. This principle implies that all other legal norms are subordinate to it, and any law that contradicts it lacks validity [8, 9]. Supremacy manifests in two dimensions: **material** and **formal** [8]. Material supremacy refers to the content of the Constitution, preventing the enactment of internal norms that oppose its provisions and objectives. Formal supremacy, for its part, ensures that the procedure for the creation of legal norms conforms to what is constitutionally established. **Constitutional rigidity** reinforces this principle, requiring more complex reform procedures than those for ordinary laws, which prevents the legislative power from altering it at will [9]. Article 31 of the National Constitution explicitly enshrines this supremacy, declaring that the Constitution, national laws enacted in consequence thereof, and international treaties are the supreme law of the country, to which provincial authorities must conform [8].

However, constitutional supremacy is not a static concept and can be affected by interpretations that distort its meaning or by the growing internationalization of law, where supranational norms and organizations can overlap with local constitutional provisions [9]. This poses a tension: How can the Constitution be supreme if it is constantly adapting? Supremacy, in this context, is not absolute but a dynamic supremacy that must be continually reaffirmed and reinterpreted in light of changing realities and the primary objective of the common good. The challenge lies in preserving the foundational authority of the Constitution while allowing for its necessary adaptation, preventing it from becoming an immovable relic or a "paper constitution" without real validity [8]. This balance between fidelity to foundational principles and pragmatic responsiveness to social needs is crucial.

3.2 Role in structuring the state's legal system

The Constitution is the fundamental pillar upon which the rule of law is built, acting as the "formal cause" of the entire legal system. It establishes **nomocracy**, or the government of law, where all state action must derive from constitutionally provided powers. Its central role is to diagram the basic powers of the state (legislative, executive, judicial, constituent, and electoral), defining their decision-making processes, their implementation, and their coordination [7, 8]. The Constitution not only organizes power but also delimits the powers of the state against the rights of individuals, establishing the principle of non-delegation of tasks assigned to each organ. In a democratic constitutional system, the individual is the "cause, foundation, and end" of all political organization. The creation and subsistence of the state, along with all its techniques and procedures, have as their exclusive purpose the realization of human liberty and dignity. This perspective implies that the Constitution is more than a regulatory document; it is a true "plan for the flourishing" of society. Its structural elements, such as the separation of powers and the normative hierarchy, are not mere administrative arrangements but are designed to create a conducive environment where human dignity and liberty can be continuously realized and enriched. The legal system, therefore, is conceived as a means to a human-centered end, ensuring that the state serves the people and not vice versa. This vision transforms the perception from a purely legalistic framework to a dynamic and purpose-oriented one.

3.3 Constitutional mechanisms for achieving the common good

The Constitution establishes a series of essential legal mechanisms to ensure the achievement of the common good.

3.3.1 The separation and control of powers

The **separation of powers** is a fundamental principle of constitutionalism, whose purpose is to prevent the concentration and abusive exercise of power, thereby safeguarding human liberty and dignity. The classical system distributes the functions of state power among the legislative, executive, and judicial branches, which operate independently but in coordination. In addition to this triad, the Argentine Constitution has incorporated new bodies such as the General Audit Office of the Nation, the Ombudsman, and the Council of the Magistracy, which, although independent, are integrated into the sphere of existing powers [4, 7, 8].

This scheme generates a system of **checks and balances**, which includes horizontal controls (intra- and inter-organ) and vertical controls (between government and society). **Horizontal intra-organ controls** manifest in the internal organization of each power, such as bicameralism in the legislative branch or collegial courts in the judiciary. **Horizontal inter-organ controls** occur between the different powers, such as the power of Congress to impeach the president or judges, the presidential veto of laws, or the judicial review exercised by the judiciary over legislative and executive acts [10]. **Vertical controls** include federalism, guarantees of individual liberties, and pluralism [8]. **Federalism**, by decentralizing political power between the federal state and the provinces, limits the authority of the central government [7–9]. **Guarantees of individual liberties** establish mechanisms to prevent government action from denaturing human dignity and liberty, such as *amparo*, *habeas data*, or the inviolability of domicile. **Social pluralism**, manifested through interest groups, political parties, and public opinion, acts as a counterweight that influences decisions and supervises the exercise of power; freedom of the press, in particular, is a strategic vertical control that ensures information and criticism of the government [4, 8].

3.3.2 Recognition and protection of fundamental rights

Fundamental rights are inherent to the human person and not a concession by the state. The Constitution recognizes and protects them, considering them expressions of human dignity. The "right to life," although not always explicitly stated, is understood as a fundamental attribute, since without it, humanity, along with liberty and dignity, cannot exist. The constitutionalist movement seeks precisely to ensure the validity of these rights and human dignity, implementing techniques that prevent such postulates from becoming illusory. This system of rights implies a reciprocity of rights and obligations, where the state and individuals have duties toward those who hold rights [1].

3.3.3 Reasonable limitations and the principle of reasonableness

Constitutional liberties, although fundamental, are not absolute; they are "essentially limited and controllable." Their exercise must harmonize with the rights of others and with the aims of the political organization. The **principle of legality** establishes that no one can be forced to do what the law does not command, nor deprived of what it does not prohibit, thus seeking individual security and predictability [8].

Complementary to legality, the **principle of reasonableness** requires that laws be "just" or "reasonable" in their mandates and prohibitions [4]. This principle is equivalent to the guarantee of "substantive due process" and seeks to preserve the value of justice in all acts of power. Article 28 of the National Constitution enshrines it by prohibiting regulatory laws from "altering" principles, rights, and guarantees.

Police power is the governmental authority to establish reasonable regulations over individual liberties to promote general welfare, public order, morality, health, and safety. It is not an arbitrary power but must be exercised by a competent body, be proportional to the aims of general interest, respond to a real need, be generic, and not nullify constitutional liberty. The recognition of fundamental rights and the imposition of reasonable limitations, along with police power, are not contradictory elements but a sophisticated mechanism for achieving the common good. If rights were absolute, they could generate conflicts and social chaos, undermining the common good. If limits were arbitrary, liberty would be nullified. The principle of reasonableness acts as the crucial balancing tool, ensuring that limitations on rights are legitimate and proportionate, serving the broader objective of the common good without distorting the essence of individual liberty. This creates a dynamic equilibrium where individual flourishing is maximized within a framework that allows for collective well-being. The common good is not achieved by sacrificing individual rights but by harmonizing them through reasonable regulation (**Table 3**).

Mechanism	Function for the common good	Examples/sub-mechanisms
Separation and control of powers	Prevent abuse of power, safeguard liberty, and ensure accountability.	Horizontal controls (intra-organ, inter-organ); vertical controls (federalism, pluralism, freedom of the press).
Recognition and protection of fundamental rights	Guarantee the inherent dignity and liberty of individuals, and create conditions for integral human development.	Civil, political, and social rights; principle of reciprocity in rights and duties.
Reasonable limitations and the principle of reasonableness	Harmonize individual rights with collective interests, avoid arbitrariness, and ensure justice in the application of the law.	Police power, Art. 28 (not altering rights by regulation), "*in dubio pro libertate*."

Table 3.
Mechanisms of Power for the Attaiment of the Common Good.

4. The indissoluble interconnection: Political program and legal system in service of the common good

4.1 Human dignity and liberty as the central axis

In a personalist system, the supreme objective of all governmental and human activity is the full realization of human liberty and dignity. All legal and political instruments are designed to make this goal achievable. Liberty is conceived in an integral manner, encompassing political, economic, and philosophical spheres. Political liberty implies the capacity to elect rulers and participate in political activity; economic liberty, based on private property, fosters human creativity and social welfare; and philosophical liberty promotes understanding, tolerance, the responsible exercise of freedoms, and respect for human dignity. The interdependence of these liberties is crucial, as the absence of one deprives the others of meaning, potentially leading to authoritarianism [1, 8].

The common good, from this perspective, presents itself as the "ideal and political project" that unifies a nation and mobilizes its citizens, preventing social fragmentation. It is the "end of all political society and also its constitutive principle" [11]. Its *raison d'être* is to serve the human person and social groups, facilitating the unfolding of their "enormous possibilities." The common good is not an abstract concept, but the social condition that allows and maximizes the integral liberty and dignity of each person. It is the framework within which individual rights are not only protected but fully developed in a collective context. This generates a virtuous cycle: A robust common good fosters individual liberty, which in turn contributes to a richer and more complete common good.

4.2 Constitutional interpretation as a tool for effectiveness

Constitutional technique is the rational procedure that allows for the application of the principles of constitutional law in the drafting and interpretation of the fundamental law [8]. It is an art, both political and legal, that seeks to amalgamate principles to structure the normative framework of a community. History shows that "professorial constitutionalism," being too theoretical and detached from reality, has led to the failure of many constitutions. This underscores the need for realism in constitutional formulation and interpretation, which considers the political, social, economic, cultural, and historical realities of the people. Interpretation must synthesize the facts of the present with the ideals of society.

Teleological or finalist interpretation is essential, as it seeks the ultimate purpose of the Constitution, which is the dominant political idea of society. In a democracy, this purpose is the limitation and control of power to safeguard human liberty and dignity. All norms must be interpreted in harmony with this overarching goal. When conflicts of legal values arise, the supreme court prioritizes interests that have "greater public interest." "General welfare," equated with the "common good" of classical philosophy, is considered the supreme value, guiding interpretation toward the achievement of justice in its highest expression [9].

Effective interpretation, especially dynamic and teleological interpretation oriented toward the common good, is not just a legal exercise but a political act of legitimization. By adapting the Constitution to changing realities without betraying its essential values (dignity, liberty, common good), interpreters ensure that the document remains a "living" and "respected" symbol, preventing it from becoming a mere "piece of paper" [8]. This continuous process of interpretation is vital to maintaining the social contract and public trust in the constitutional order.

4.3 Challenges and future perspectives

The Constitution, despite its noble purposes, faces a "critical situation" in attempting to "reduce the existing separation between the norm and reality." There will always be a "margin of distortion" between the constitutional order (the ought to be) and the political order (the being) [8]. To overcome this gap, **civic education** is fundamental. The effectiveness of democratic constitutional systems depends on the "cultural and educational level" of society. Civic education is indispensable for citizens to understand their role, their responsibilities, and the transcendence of the Constitution and its values. Without it, the people run the risk of being a "mass" instead of a conscious and active "nation" [10].

Likewise, the "ethical example of rulers" is crucial for the Constitution to function as a "national symbol" and an "instrument of government." Inconsistency in the conduct of political leaders can erode public trust and the legitimacy of the system. The history of constitutionalism is a "permanent struggle of man for liberty" against totalitarian and authoritarian doctrines. This struggle persists, with the emergence of new neo-authoritarian tendencies [8]. This suggests that the Constitution is not a finished product but a social project in constant construction. Its effectiveness in achieving the common good is not guaranteed by its mere existence or even by its perfect wording. It requires a continuous effort from both rulers (through ethical conduct and faithful application) and the governed (through civic responsibility and informed participation). The Constitution provides the framework and ideals, but its realization is a perpetual effort, an "ascending march" toward a more just and free society [8]. The common good, in this sense, is a horizon to which one constantly aspires, not a fixed destination.

5. Conclusion

The Constitution reveals itself as an integral instrument that, through its political program and legal system, pursues the common good of individuals. As a political program, it articulates the vision of the nation, its fundamental aims, and the ideal of communitarian personalism, which balances individual dignity with human sociability. As a legal system, it establishes a robust normative framework based on constitutional supremacy, the separation and control of powers, and the recognition of fundamental rights with reasonable limitations, all designed to guarantee order and justice. Both dimensions are intrinsically directed toward the achievement of the common good, with human dignity and liberty as supreme objectives. The dynamic nature of the Constitution, especially through teleological and systematic interpretation, is crucial for its adaptation to changing social realities and for maintaining its relevance and effectiveness. However, the materialization of these ideals is a continuous challenge, requiring constant vigilance, the civic education of citizens, and the ethical example of rulers. The Constitution, ultimately, is not a mere text but a living project and a national symbol that explains the aims of society and serves as an instrument of government that must be faithfully fulfilled for the full validity of a rule of law. The common good, therefore, is a perpetual aspiration that requires constant commitment to close the gap between the constitutional ideal and lived reality.

Author details

Nicolás Jorge Negri
University of Palermo, Buenos Aires, Argentina

*Address all correspondence to: njnster@gmail.com

References

[1] Bidart Campos G. Manual de la Constitución Reformada. Buenos Aires: EDIAR. Vol. **I and II**; 2006.

[2] Ekmekdjian MA. Tratado de Derecho Constitucional. Buenos Aires: La Ley; 2016.

[3] Loewenstein K. Teoría de la Constitución. Barcelona: Ariel; 1986.

[4] Manili PL. Tratado de Derecho Constitucional Argentino Y Comparado. Buenos Aires: La Ley. 2nd Vol. **I**; 2024.

[5] Nino CS. Fundamentos de Derecho Constitucional. Buenos Aires: Astrea; 1992.

[6] Rosatti H. Tratado de Derecho Constitucional Santa Fe Rubinzal-Culzoni. 2025.

[7] Santiago A. Lecciones de Derecho Constitucional. Buenos Aires: Universidad Austral Ediciones. Vol. **I**; 2025. 2024.

[8] Badeni G. Tratado de Derecho Constitucional. Buenos Aires: La Ley. 2nd Vol. **I**; 2006.

[9] Sagüés NP. Manual de Derecho Constitucional. 3rd ed. Buenos Aires: Astrea; 2019.

[10] González JV. Manual de la Constitución Argentina. Ángel Estrada Y Cía. Buenos Aires: Editores; 1897.

[11] Santiago A. Bien Común y derecho constitucional. Buenos Aires: Ábaco; 2002.

Chapter 4

Evolutionary Interpretation in Constitutional Law: Between Accommodation and Instrumentalization

Jarosław Szymanek

Abstract

The article addresses the issue of constitutional interpretation. The starting point is the assumption that constitutional interpretation is a continuous process, as the constitution is essentially created or constructed through its interpretations (which vary greatly). We can discuss judicial interpretation, legislative interpretation (which involves developing the text of the constitution through legislation), and practical interpretation (which pertains to the behavioral application of the constitution by political actors). A separate issue is the interpretation made by constitutional law doctrine, for which a more appropriate term is "commentary." Various techniques are employed in the interpretation process. These include linguistic interpretation, functional interpretation, purposive interpretation, and historical interpretation, for example. However, all these techniques must adhere to one basic principle: they must be consistent with the constitution and pro-constitutional. Loyalty to the constitution (its letter and spirit) is a fundamental duty of anyone who interprets the constitution. This is why the concept of evolutionary interpretation, which is increasingly proposed in commentaries on constitutional law doctrine, is causing so much concern today. It is driven by the slogan of the progressiveness of the constitution and its adequacy to changing times. However, evolutionary interpretation is extremely dangerous, especially if its results differ from those of linguistic, historical, or functional interpretation. Therefore, the proposal of evolutionary interpretation should be approached with great caution. It lies between the obvious need to adapt the constitution and the dangerous temptation to instrumentalize it.

Keywords: constitution, constitutional disputes, interpretation, accommodations, instrumentalization, constitutional jurisprudence, constitutional law doctrine

1. Introduction

Constitutional interpretation is a natural and ongoing process. There is no constitution in the world that is not subject to interpretation. This allows the constitution to adapt to the changing context of its application, making it a living constitution, not just a formal constitution, a constitution "in book" or a "worthless piece of paper." The latter case is illustrated, at best, by authoritarian states, in whose reality constitutions are merely mock-ups that conceal the ugliness of the system and the real decision-making mechanisms, which most often have nothing to do with democracy, the rule of law, or the reliability of public institutions.

Only the constitutions of authoritarian satrapies and more or less open dictatorships do not need interpretation, because in practice they have no meaning and are not applied, which, however, is also a kind of their "some" interpretation — interpretation *à rebours* — according to the logic that the lack of interpretation, the lack of adaptation to circumstances, to the emerging, often changing situational contexts, is also a form of interpretation, because regardless of everything, the constitution is applied there in one, top-down and possible way. The lack of openness of authoritarian constitutions to true, creative interpretation results from the fact that they are merely curtains or screens, often beautiful, lofty, and super-democratic in their verbal form, which cover up the thoroughly flawed and non-transparent mechanisms of state operation, for which there is often not even a constitutional model.

However, in a proper democracy, a constitution is not only a concrete fact (a legal act) but also a process — that is, a sequence of actions, various ways of reading it, and applying it in practice. This means that, *nolens volens*, the constitution is subject to permanent interpretation, occurring at very different levels. Some even believe that only a complex, multivector process of constitutional interpretation creates a proper constitution, which is not only its literal text but also all its variants, taking the form of appropriate constitutional practice, judicial interpretation (performed primarily, but not exclusively, by constitutional courts), or doctrinal interpretation, which, on a daily basis, engages in a specific commentary on the constitution and offers optimal methods of its application depending on emerging needs and circumstances. According to this view, the constitution, before the process of its interpretation, is only a certain plastic material that does not yet have its final form, because this is given slowly, gradually, in the process of interpreting the constitution — that is, reading its detailed content and deriving norms from general, sometimes even catchword-like provisions.

As a result, every democratic, effectively binding constitution is interpreted through its practical application, judicial interpretation, and doctrinal commentary, responding to emerging problems and challenges. Practical interpretation is a method of applying constitutional norms by so-called constitutional actors, that is, entities obliged to apply the constitution (parliamentarians, members of the government, the president). Judicial interpretation, officially made in the name and on behalf of the state, acquires the status of court decisions, that is, common courts, administrative courts, and – especially – constitutional courts, which are particularly entitled to express their views on how the constitution should be interpreted so that it is fully respected and thus recognized as an authentic act, not just an apparent one. Practical and judicial interpretation, however, never occurs in a vacuum, as their background is always doctrinal interpretation, meaning the views of legal scholars and various pronouncements of legal authorities, which are confirmed case by case either in constitutional practice (practical interpretation) or in court rulings, which elevate the approved views of legal doctrine to the rank of judicial decisions, establishing binding patterns of conduct with constitutional status. In either case, there is no democratic, truly binding constitution that is immune to interpretation.

2. Interpretation as a method of creating a constitution

It is a truism that the constitution, however defined, is subject to interpretation. Interpretation is an inherent element of the constitution[1] [1], to such an extent that without interpretation, the very concept of the constitution is subject to erosion, that it loses its elementary meaning, and even – as Michel Troper says – ontologically ceases to exist[2] [2]. For the French researcher, there is no inherent, universal, and above all, *ex proprio vigore* meaning of the constitution. It is given, created, or shaped only as a result of interpretation, and interpretation understood in the plural, because just as there is no constitution without interpretation, there is no single, universal, and constant interpretation, and there are many possible ways of reading the constitution, or as M. Troper would like to put it – of constructing it[3] [3]. Interpretations are therefore a specific causative power of the constitution; they are – as M. Troper says – a tool for constituting the constitution through its application[4] [2]. This, in turn – *nolens volens* – brings to mind the key thesis of Pierre Bourdieu's thought, according to which law, including the constitution, is primarily a social fact, which is not so much created thanks to the fiat of the legislator, but rather is in a constant state of *nascendi,* taking place thanks to the confrontation of agents equipped with social and technical competence consisting in the socially recognized and accepted ability to interpret, in a more or less freeway, the body of legal texts approving a valid vision of the social world, considered desirable and appropriate[5] [4]. This is also complemented by the well-known Bourdieusian concept of habitus, which plays a significant role in the process of this decoding, and which consists of the acquired skills and competences of an individual, which take the form of permanent dispositions such as ways of perceiving the world or rules of action and thinking, which are not constant in nature and therefore change (sometimes very frequently). Habitus therefore goes beyond both automatic determinism and free, unfettered will. It is precisely in the non-discursive nature of habitus that we can see the reasons for uncontrolled changes in the structure of behavior, including those related to the application of law, including the constitution. The latter, according to P. Bourdieu, creates a sequence of "unintentional invention and controlled improvisation," which, by the way, best proves that the constitution is, above all, a social fact, not a legal fact, a dynamic and unstable fact, not a stable and unchanging one[6] [5].

As a result, interpretations of the constitution differ in the material sense (i.e., the principles, rules, norms, and values derived from it) as well as in the formal sense, as they may take the form of legislative, judicial, doctrinal, or finally "behavioral" interpretation, that is, externalized by the practice of applying the legal act, which, especially in the case of the constitution, plays a very important and sometimes even decisive role. This brings to mind the old truth that although the text of the

---

[1] Just like any other law, which has always been with us. For more on this topic, see: B. Frydman, *Le sens des lois: Histoire de l'interprétation et de la raison juridique*, Paris 2011, *passim.*

[2] M. Troper, *L'interprétation constitutionnelle*, In: *L'interprétation constitutionnelle*, ed. F. Mélin-Soucramanien, Paris 2005, p. 20, 21.

[3] Por. J. Derrida, *Law, Justice and Interpretation*, New York 2006, *passim.*

[4] M. Troper, *L'interprétation constitutionnelle..*, p. 20.

[5] P. Bourdieu, L. Wacquant, *La force du droit: éléments pour une sociologie du champ juridique*, "Actes de la Recherche en Sciecnes Sociales" 1986, no 64, p. 4.

[6] B. Dupret, *Droit et sciences sociales. Pour une respécification praxéologique*, "Droit et Société" 2010, no 2, p.315–335.

constitution itself has special legal force, it does not have any special causative power. The latter is the case with narratives and interpretations that introduce the dry text of a legal act into social circulation and thus determine its sense and meaning each time. This view is not an isolated one, and it strongly resonates with the position of Pierre Legendre, for example, according to whom the textual constitution itself is nothing more than a shapeless mass, a dead text, whose resurrection and subsequent introduction into social reality takes place with the participation of various narratives, interpretations, and compilations, driven by the ambiguity and axiological capacity of the signs encoded in the text of the constitutional document. Consequently, as P. Legendre says, only the commentary, only the exegesis of the constitution gives the *corps constitutionnel*, creating in its entirety a refined constitutional dialectic[7] [6]. For P. Legendre, the constitution is therefore an amorphous entity, given its proper form only by interpretations, which in turn are animated and motivated by the polysemy of signs, which, in the case of the constitution, takes the form of a virtual exaggeration. The literal constitution, after all, is full of concepts and phrases that are vague, unstable, flexible, and capacious enough to require concretization and clarification. The entropy of the terminology used by the author of the constitution requires obvious intervention in the form of appropriate clarification, specification, and interpretation. Without all these efforts, the constitution would be just a piece of paper without any significant meaning, which means that it would not be able to fulfill all the functions assigned to it, which means that, as a socio-political entity, it would essentially be annihilated, becoming at most a fictitious or apparent constitution. Interpretations of the constitution are therefore an obligatory element of its very existence, and especially of the socio-political operation of the constitution, an element without which the constitution becomes a Lovensteinian semantic constitution, which in no way determines the rules of operation of the political system, because these have a completely different course and are determined by other factors.

If we take the position that, without (different) interpretations, the concept of a constitution means nothing, then the statement often made by constitutionalists — that a constitution is not immutable, that it changes, that it evolves, that although, in the sense of a textual unit, it remains the same, thanks to its interpretations, it is never the same — becomes obvious, even banal. Therefore, the substrate for deconstructing the content of the norm (i.e., the pattern of the required, prescribed, or prohibited behavior of the addressees of the law) remains unchanged at most, but the norm itself – as a pattern of specific conduct – is, at least in some sense, changeable or at least ambiguous, which results from the fact that it is always the result of specific intellectual procedures consisting in the correct (or only perceived as such) way of reading the relevant textual unit. The process of interpreting the constitution is therefore not so much a process of simple reading of the constitution (which supposedly exists *per se ipse* without any interpretative procedures) but rather a process of its permanent creation, or perhaps rather "discovery." It consists in the fact that, as a result of interpretation, there is only an actual (real) creation of norms that are only potentially present in the textual layer of the constitution[8] [7]. The latter is therefore only the material for the constitution, the rudimentary meaning of which is much broader, as it covers the process of decoding — using various exponential techniques — the content contained both explicitly and – above all – implicitly in the

[7] P. Legendre, *L'amour du conseur. Essai sur l'orde dogmatique*, Paris 1974, p. 81.

[8] Y. Aguila, *Cinq questions sur l'interpretation constitutionnelle*, „Revue Francaise de Droit Constitutionell" 1995, no 21, p. 30.

base material, that is, the text of the constitution itself (also referred to as the formal or textual constitution). That is why, opposite to it, the concept of a material constitution appeared, complementary to the formal constitution and, at the same time, obligatory for it. It proves best that only the combined juxtaposition of the formal and material approach (meaning) of the constitution gives a proper, comprehensive, full, or complete constitution. While the formal constitution is the textual substrate of the constitution itself, the material constitution is the specific norms, principles, rules, and values – decoded on the basis of the formal constitution – and, alongside them, the method of their practical application – which is extremely important because it can go in various directions. The material constitution, or – as M. Troper would say – the constitution *tout court,* is therefore created through the application of very different interpretative procedures, encompassing the activity of courts, including constitutional courts, the activity of the legislator who details and materializes the provisions contained in the text of the constitution, but also the findings of the doctrine and, finally – last but not least – constitutional practice. All this, in slightly different terminology, constitutes the so-called constitution in action, which, in the traditional doctrine of constitutional law, constitutes a counterpoint to the constitution in book, that is, the source material that constitutes the subject of exegesis, making the constitution real and "living."

Of course, for the aforementioned Michel Troper, the indicated distinction is completely irrelevant because, according to him, there is no constitution in the book, but at most an element, a component, or an element of it, which becomes the proper constitution only when it is interpreted (understood very broadly, by the way). In any case, each of these positions assumes that interpretation is a relevant factor in the constitution. The only difference between them is that Michel Troper orthodoxly assumes that without interpretation, there simply is no constitution, because only interpretations transform a potential existence into an actual existence, while the other two positions emphasize only the incompleteness or fragmentation of a constitution if the element of its interpretation is not taken into account. Hence, the category of a substantive constitution (as a complement to the formal constitution) or a constitution in action, which is intended to complement the constitution in the book. Nevertheless, all these initial concepts undoubtedly converge in one thing, namely that interpretations of the constitution are an inseparable element of the constitution and either construct it (according to Michel Troper) or co-shape or complement it to a very significant extent. By the way, adopting such an assumption makes all kinds of speculations about what we actually mean when we talk about the constitution obsolete. This type of speculation is eagerly and frequently engaged in by the traditional science of constitutional law, which can understand a constitution as either a literal constitution (the text of the constitution), a so-called judicial constitution (i.e., the result of the interpretation of courts, especially constitutional courts), a practical or real constitution (emphasizing the actual way of updating constitutional norms by entities applying the constitution), or finally a so-called doctrinal constitution (i.e., the result of the exegesis of the constitution performed by the doctrine of constitutional law)[9] [8]. It seems that these various constitutions are, in fact, at

[9] This type of distinction is also followed by a distinction between constitutional amendments, which may take the form of a proper amendment, i.e. a change interfering with the text of the constitution, a judicial (judicial) change, a practical change or a doctrinal change. For more on this topic, see: K.C. Wheare, *Modern Constitutions*, London – New York – Toronto 1967, p. 83 and next.

most fragments of the constitution or its puzzles, which only when put together give a complete picture of the constitution, which is always a synergy of the elements that compose it (in which M. Troper is undoubtedly right). Therefore, when speaking about an authentic constitution, one should have in mind the belief that a proper constitution is created when the starting point, which is the text of the constitutional document, is interpreted thanks to the detailed activity of the ordinary legislator, court decisions, explanations of the doctrine, and – last but not least – practical mechanisms of applying the constitution[10] [9]. Without all this, we cannot sensibly answer the question of what the constitution looks like, and therefore what the actual mechanisms of the political game look like. This is confirmed by extreme examples – on the one hand – the US Constitution, and on the other, everything that made up the literal constitution of the French Third Republic. In each of these cases, and these are particularly acute cases, the text of the constitution itself not only says nothing about the content of the *corps constitutionnel* – as P. Legendre would say – but can deform and distort this content. Moreover, in both cases, the constitutional document has a completely secondary, even marginal, significance for the actual, de facto constitution – understood as the dialectic of relations between state organs and the comfort of individual rights and freedoms.

3. Different approaches to interpretation

Accepting the initial assumption that interpretations of the constitution are an indispensable element of it, in turn, forces us to ask a fundamental question about what the act of interpreting the constitution actually is. It can be understood either according to the concept of the act of knowledge (*l'acte de connaissance*) or according to the concept of the act of will (*l'acte de volonté*)[11] [10].

The first of these concepts attempts to objectify the interpretation of the constitution, giving it fully scientific features, which also means that it is subject to specific, clear, and understandable rules of verification or falsification. This type of interpretation is typical of the positivist approach, based on the epistemological foundations of cognitivism, where the act of decoding the text of the constitution is purely descriptive and secondary. According to its assumptions, the basic meaning of a statement exists prior to interpretation and can be objectively known through appropriate methods of interpretation, which are reconstructive and not creative in relation to it[12] [11]. The techniques of subjective interpretation, which refer to the intentions of the legislator, and the techniques of objective interpretation, which refer to the postulate of coherence of law and its rationality, are of crucial importance here[13] [7]. According to this concept, the entity interpreting the constitution

---

10 M. Troper, *L'interprétation constitutionnelle..*, p. 22.

11 P. Delnoy, *Elements de méthodologie juridique: Méthodologie de l'interprétation juridique. Méthodologie de l'application du droit*, Liège 2005, *passim*.

12 This issue is also of particular interest to the doctrine of Polish constitutional law and other post-communist countries, where the need to interpret the constitution in the process of democratic transformation has very often arisen. For more on this topic, see: R. Sarkowicz, *Uwagi o współczesnej interpretacji prawniczej*, [in:] *Polska kultura prawna a proces integracji europejskiej*, ed. S. Wronkowska, Kraków 2005, p. 11 and next.

13 Y. Aguila, *Cinq questions sur l'interpretation..*, p. 24,25.

(whether legislative, behavioral, or judicial) does not so much add something new to the content of the norm or – even more so – create a new state of constitutional regulation, but rather specifies, makes real, and above all externalizes this state by explicating the decoded content of the constitution, which allows for the translation of the language of law into the language of practice. The author of an interpretative decision is, according to this concept, a sage who uses his glass and eye to read the meaning encoded in the complex content of a constitutional act. However, their role is solely to interpret the meaning and explain it, and – if necessary – justify it, and not to create something new, for example, create law. Law – according to this concept – exists objectively and requires only explanatory procedures, and this is precisely what interpretation is for.

The second concept, on the other hand, assumes that interpretation is, by its nature, an act of will. This means that the entity interpreting the constitution (or, in M. Troper's terms, constructing it) is not subject to any objective — let alone strictly scientific — rules, and therefore has a very large margin of freedom in determining the meaning of the text contained in the constitution in the book. Moreover, this margin increases because, in interpretation as a typical act of will, justification, explanation, and, in some cases — and these are by no means rare — even creation dominate over the proper reconstruction of the meaning of the content of the constitution. Interpretation here is, therefore, a creative and not a reproducible activity, an activity that treats the constitutional material as a kind of plastic mass from which law, in the proper or strict sense of the word, will emerge. As M. Troper, already quoted here many times, points out, interpretation understood as an act of will is primarily intended to justify a posteriori the views of the interpreting subject, who, in turn, creates them on the basis of his subjective assessments and judgments. We are not dealing here, as the concept of the act of cognition would have it, with the independent and objective — and above all, almost atavistic — existence of a norm, but with its reconstruction, which, in each case, precedes the adoption of a predetermined vision of the interpretative direction. This, in itself, also undermines the veil of ignorance and impartiality inherent in the concept of interpretation as an act of cognition, which is supposed to be the share of the glossator. This means that, in the concept of interpretation as an act of will, the context of justification prevails over the context of discovering or deriving a model of the appropriate behavior of the addressee of constitutional norms. This is facilitated by a whole range of constitutional interpretation tools (e.g., linguistic, teleological, functional, systemic interpretation) or – in a different convention – originalism or textualism. Nowadays, there is an increasing willingness to resort to the so-called evolutionary interpretation, which can be considered the quintessence of understanding constitutional interpretation as an act of will. In many cases, particularly creative readings of the constitutional text, evolutionary interpretation is considered to precede all other methods of interpretation, even when linguistic, functional, or, for example, teleological interpretations yield satisfactory results. Thanks to this, and the freedom to use various interpretation techniques, interpretation as an act of will allows for "easily justifying any interpretative decision, which gives the interpreter a great deal of intellectual freedom"[14] [12]. The freedom to use arguments, determined by a previously formed assessment and view, means that the entity interpreting the constitution de facto uses "eclectic tactics" (*l'éclectisme tactique*), which, in practice, means the freedom

[14] K.J. Kaleta, *Wykładnia prawa jako forma włączy politycznej. Stanowiska wobec interpretacji konstytucji w doktrynie francuskiej*, [in:] *Wykładnia konstytucji. Inspiracje, teorie, argumenty*, ed. T. Stawecki, J. Winczorek, Warszawa 2014, p. 73.

to use various justifications for interpretative decisions[15] [13]. In this way, the interpretation itself is transformed into nothing more than a juggling of "interpretive tools" chosen not to explain the meaning of the norm *erga omnes*, but to create it in the way the author of the interpretative decision had previously intended (which completely undermines the assumption of the objectivity and impartiality of the exegete, which, after all, is the foundation of the concept of interpretation as *l'acte de volonté*). Hence, according to this concept, each interpretation has a creative but, at the same time, highly subjective character, which is a natural perpetual motion of subsequent exponential procedures[16] [14]. The interpreter of the constitution does not so much read its rudimentary and, at most, implicit meaning but creates the meaning — creates, like a demiurge – a new legal reality, multiplying the claim to be not only an exegete but also a legislator, and even – in some cases – a constitutional maker, using the arsenal of arguments provided by the history of the narrative about the state, law, and politics, and which constitutes a material source for all interpretative procedures[17] [15]. The act of interpretation here is not just a simple narrative about the already existing law, but it is an act of introducing a new norm into the legal system, ergo a new legal state, correcting the status quo (which – let us note – overturns the paradigm of the traditional legislator). In this type of interpretative activity, the exegete crosses the Rubicon of the sage and grows into the role of a priest and creator of a new (changed) order of things, ultimately creating, together with other entities, a multicentric constitutionalist system in which the content of the constitution (understood in the manner of M. Troper) is decided by a great many entities involved in the constitutional process, both at the stage of its enactment and application (which distinction simultaneously loses its fundamental meaning)[18] [16]. Moreover, each such interpretation introduces the volitional factor of politics into the concept of the constitution, which thus becomes an inseparable component of the concept of the constitution, treated much more broadly as *droit politique*[19] [17], where the logic of legal positivism is mixed with the empiricism of political science[20] [18].

This is precisely the essence of the complexity of the constitution and its interpretation. While the text of the constitution itself is the legal (juridical) substrate of the constitution (broadly understood), its interpretations are the political substrate of that constitution. This makes the constitution, especially understood in the manner of M. Troper, the subject of a political game, but one conducted in a specific, sophisticated way, using means of an obviously legal nature[21] [7]. In this way, law and politics are mixed, and this creates a special kind of entity — the constitution — which is a complex document in which various layers are compiled (political, historical, legal, ideological, axiological, sociological, and even moral)[22] [19]. It generates, understandably, the complexity of the issue of constitutional interpretation

[15] J. Carbonnier, *Droit civil*, Paris 2004, p. 288.

[16] M. Troper, *Le problème de l'interprétation et la théorie de la supralégalité constitutionnel*, [in:] *Recueil d'étude en hommage Charles Eisenmann*, Paris 1975, p. 147.

[17] S. Goyard-Fabre, *Les principes philospohique du droit politique moderne*, Paris 1997, p. 401.

[18] P. Jan, *Le procès constitutionnel*, Paris 2010, p. 187 and next.

[19] E.-P. Guiselin, *Le droit de la vie politique*, Paris 2004, p. 77.

[20] J. Chevallier, *Droit et politique*, Paris 1993, p. 255 and next.

[21] Y. Aguila, *Cinq questions sur l'interpretation..*, p. 14.

[22] Especially in the French doctrine it is treated as a political act, or at least as a dual, legal-political act, a mixed act. For more on this topic, see: D. Rousseau, *Question de constitution*, [in:] *Le nouveau constitutionnalisme. Mélanges en l'honneur de Gérard Conac*, ed. J.-C. Colliard, Y. Jegouzo, Paris 2001, p. 3 and next.

because, firstly, it introduces an openly political (volitional) element into the constitution, and secondly, it ideologizes the constitution, whose phrases and terms not only are capacious and unstable in their content but also characterized by a very high degree of value judgment, and this is never politically indifferent or irrelevant. This, among other things, means that interpretations of the constitution, like interpretations of any other legal act, are susceptible or even favorable toward interpretations other than strictly judicial ones. While in other branches of law, judicial interpretation is understandably dominant and is generally considered the primary mechanism for interpreting the law, the situation is somewhat different in the case of the constitution. Legislative interpretation, meaning the interpretation that translates general and sometimes even vague constitutional provisions into the language of statutory norms, is of crucial importance (the significance of which increases with the generality of the constitutional text). A significant role is also played by the "behavioral" interpretation, which involves the practical application of constitutional norms by participants in political relations. This often not only implements and specifies the vague or even incomplete provisions of the textual constitution but even supplements them. Finally, doctrinal interpretation plays a very important role, as it provides commentary on both the legislative and behavioral interpretation, which in turn constitutes an advantage for the findings made by judicial interpretation[23] [20]. The latter, especially until constitutional courts become more widespread, is becoming increasingly important. Firstly, because statistically it begins to clearly dominate all other forms of reconstructing the text of the constitution. Secondly, because it claims to be the only authoritative interpretation of the text of the constitution, devaluing all other methods of decoding it. Thirdly, because it introduces an overtly political element into classical judicial interpretation, which significantly alters the very concept of constitutional courts, giving them the appearance of a political court *par excellence*[24] [21]. Fourthly, and finally, because it reorients the current model of applying the constitution, blurring the clear divisions between the proper application of law and its enactment. The interpretation made by the constitutional court also best reveals the previously mentioned tension between the understanding of an interpretation as an act of cognition and an act of will. Constitutional jurisprudence, depending on the case and circumstances, falls more into the concept of an act of cognition or more into the concept of an act of will. This first concept, understandably, disciplines the constitutional court by responding to the vision of so-called judicial passivism. In contrast, the concept of perceiving interpretation as an act of will pushes the constitutional court toward activism, which is today one of the most discussed issues in the science of constitutional law. This is because it is the best exemplification of the cross-border nature of this law in almost all its aspects, that is, the demarcation between law and politics or the demarcation between law-making and its application. The increasingly active stance of the constitutional judiciary obviously has much broader implications. It is significantly changing the process of constitutional interpretation, including through the perceived

[23] Y. Poimeur, D. Rosenberg, *La doctrine constitutionnelle et le constitutionnalisme français*, [in:] *Les usages sociaux du droit*, ed. D. Lochak, Paris 1989, p. 230 and next.

[24] It is worth recalling that also for Hans Kelsen the constitutional judiciary had a clearly political profile, which was manifested, among other things, in the fact that H. Kelsen directly called the constitutional court a political court (*cour politique*), postulating a clearly political method of electing constitutional judges, i.e. by parliament. For more on this topic, see: M. Troper, *La liberté d'interprétation du juge constitutionnel*, [in:] *Interprétation de drot*, ed. P. Amselek, Bruxelles 1995, p. 238.

deprecation of other forms of deciphering its text, but also through the redefinition of classic theories concerning, among other things, the separation of powers, the binding of judges, and the limits of adjudicative activity.

Nevertheless, even the impetus with which the jurisprudence of constitutional courts approaches the interpretation of the constitution does not change the key assumption of this interpretation, which is the relative freedom in determining the content of constitutional decisions[25] [22]. A relatively large margin of interpretation of the meaning of the constitution applies equally to, for example, an ordinary legislator who, when detailing the provisions of the constitution, adopts one of the possible ways of interpreting it, and – especially – to a practitioner who, among the possible choices of applying the content of a constitutional provision, selects one for some reasons, considering the others to be less justified or – simply – not useful. The court, including the constitutional court, although its decisions are undoubtedly much more disciplined and, above all, objectivized, also has a relative freedom of decision, which results not so much from the specificity of the constitutional court itself, but from the specificity of the act subject to its cognition. The relative freedom of interpretation, which is also at the disposal of the constitutional court, is further supported by various interpretative techniques and the fact that the court may use them with varying intensity and in different combinations, depending, among other things, on whether it wants to be more restrained or perhaps more ambitious and active.

Of course, the choice of a specific method of interpretation remains at the discretion of the court. However, there are general principles that should guide this assessment, such as giving priority to linguistic interpretation, which often yields satisfactory results in determining the content of a norm. Understandably, other methods of reconstructing the norm should only be applied as a last resort. Nevertheless, today we are increasingly seeing, encouraged by the so-called progressive doctrine of constitutional law, a tendency to adopt the so-called evolutionary interpretation regardless of everything else. Proponents of this interpretation argue that the ways of interpreting the constitution should be viewed dynamically and that one cannot be "held hostage" to a specific interpretation, for example, linguistic or functional. They assume that the constitution and the law "in general," as well as society and the whole world, are subject to natural evolution, which means that the way of looking at the constitution should also evolve. In extreme cases, it should even lead to the derivation of content from the constitution that is not present there but is supposedly "obvious" because "times have changed," "we live in a different reality," "we cannot fall into the absurdity of excessive formalism," etc. Sometimes this view is even maximized, and, referring to M. Troper's concept, it suggests that only what is derived from the constitution is the proper constitution, and the basis for it is not only the text itself but also other imperatives of thinking, and even norms that are not formally anchored in the constitution. The most progressive supporters of this thesis are even inclined to argue that only a constitution interpreted in this way is the proper constitution, and that its building blocks are the totality of beliefs, norms, and values dynamically, that is, evolutionarily interpreted by the interpreting entity.

The use of the so-called evolutionary interpretation is intended to result in even greater freedom in deriving from the constitution norms, principles, and values that we expect but for which there is no legal basis, or – at best – only a very weak one.

---

[25] R. Langlois, *L'application des règles d'interprétation constitutionnelle*, "Les Cahiers de Droit"1987, nr 1, p. 207 end next.

Supporters of this interpretation point out that it is an ideal method of adapting the constitution to rapidly changing circumstances. Opponents of evolutionary interpretation, on the other hand, are concerned about its arbitrariness, its detachment from other methods of interpreting the constitution, and the fact that, under the guise of accommodating the constitution, it proposes the instrumental use of law. For this reason, they promote the entirely valid view that any technique of constitutional interpretation should, first and foremost, meet the requirement of constitutional interpretation. Regardless of whether we use linguistic, historical, functional, systemic, or evolutionary interpretation, the result of its application must always be in accordance with the constitution. After all, we interpret the constitution in order to implement it as fully as possible, which means that any other outcome of the interpretation should lead to the rejection of the result of such an interpretation. The interpretation of the constitution cannot produce results that are inconsistent with the constitution! Of course, whether the evolutionary interpretation will find any support depends on many circumstances. It depends on who interprets the constitution, for what purpose they do so, on what basis the interpretation is made, but it also depends on the professionalism of the interpreting entity and whether that entity is more political or substantive[26] [9]. It can be assumed that if the interpreter of the constitution is more of a politician than a lawyer, they will be inclined to use the constitution instrumentally, which, in turn, means that they will be inclined to resort to evolutionary interpretation. This is often evidenced by the justification used when resorting to evolutionary interpretation. In such cases, strictly legal arguments take a back seat, as do arguments based on linguistic or historical interpretations. The *ultima ratio* of such an interpretation of the constitution is to be the "need of the moment," "historical circumstances," "progress," "the requirements of modernity," "adaptation to some universal standard," or, conversely, "the antiquity of the text of the constitution," "its incompatibility with the present day," "deviation from the model," etc. From this point of view, evolutionary interpretation is the least "legal" way of interpreting the constitution and dangerously approaches the boundary of constitutional praxeology, which is determined, on the one hand, by the need for accommodation and, on the other, by the temptation to instrumentalize.

It is clear that autonomy in interpreting the constitution also applies to which layers of the textual constitution it will concern. It can be assumed that if this intervention relates to "static" areas of constitutional regulation, the interpretative tools will be, and in practice are, different in the sense that they are more restrained, restrictive, and limiting to the activity of the interpreting entity. If, on the other hand, the constitutional court's jurisprudence touches upon a "dynamic" part of the constitution, the likelihood of applying more dynamic, creative, ambitious, and thus more actionable interpretative techniques will also increase[27] [23].

4. The practice of interpreting the constitution

The fact that the tools for interpreting the constitution are usually quite broad, allowing for more or less far-reaching interpretation (depending on the needs and

---

[26] R. Langlois, *L'application des règles d'interprétation constitutionnelle*, "Les Cahiers de Droit"1987, nr 1, p. 207 et next.

[27] For more on this topic, see: F. Delpérée, *La Constitution et son interprétation*, [in:] *L' interpretation en droit. Approche pluridisciplinaire*, ed. M. Van de Kerchove, P. Gérard, Bruxelles 1978, p. 187 and next.

circumstances), is perfectly confirmed by what is probably the most commonly used interpretative technique today, commonly referred to as "interpretation of laws in accordance with the constitution." This technique is viewed in very different ways — both critically, as a technique that gives the constitutional court excessive freedom of action, and positively, as a technique of necessary "interpretative leeway" that falls within the decision-making scope of the constitutional judiciary and is a special form of constitutional interpretation.

It is generally agreed that it is a relatively flexible interpretative instrument, in which the text of the constitution can be interpreted both passively and actively. If the so-called negative interpretation of laws in accordance with the constitution is accepted, the interpreting entity will demonstrate a restrained attitude, recognizing that the examined norm is, for example, consistent with the constitution because it falls within the scope of permissible detail of the constitutional norm, not excluded in any way *a priori*. In the case of a more active approach, a positive interpretation of the laws in accordance with the constitution will come into play, boiling down to the statement that the norm is, for example, consistent with the constitution because it properly implements the provision of the constitution, previously interpreted as the only acceptable way of reading the constitution. So, while negative interpretation means excluding any interpretation of a provision that is contrary to the constitution, positive interpretation means adopting a constitutional interpretation of a provision while excluding any other interpretation. In the first case, therefore, only those interpretations of the constitution that are unconstitutional are determined, leaving freedom to interpret other, constitutionally compliant forms of detailing the constitutional provision, while in the second case, the action is decidedly activist. It does not stop at stating that a particular interpretation of the constitution is unconstitutional (thus leaving room for other interpretations of the constitution, which are, in principle, permissible), but formulates the only authoritative form of constitutional interpretation of the provision of the basic law and, depending on its emphasis, determines the constitutionality or unconstitutionality of the assessed norms. In other words, it is a matter of prohibiting a specific interpretation in the first case and mandating a specific interpretation in the second.

It is pointed out that, especially in situations where a court, and in particular a constitutional court, resorts to a positive form of interpretation of laws, it then creatively interprets and even co-shapes the constitution, introducing into legal circulation, with universal applicability, a specific understanding of the constitution under the threat of declaring any other way of detailing and specifying a constitutional provision unconstitutional. This type of interpretation is increasingly used by courts in judicial review proceedings, and its natural "environment" is conciseness and, consequently, the capacity of constitutional formulations, which in practice can be interpreted in various ways. A large part of constitutional norms is flexible enough to be developed in various ways at the level of ordinary legislation. However, such development is not always arbitrary, and its freedom is largely conditioned by a positive or negative interpretation of laws in accordance with the constitution. Adopting a positive interpretation limits the legislator, allowing the constitutional norm to be developed in only one strictly specified manner, which, in the opinion of the constitutional court, is an acceptable form of concretization of the constitutional norm. The use of negative interpretation restricts the discretion of the court, creating a significantly greater area of legislative freedom for the ordinary legislator. As a result, the very structure of interpreting laws in accordance with the constitution gives the interpreting body a considerable margin of discretion, generating in practice what could be called a "reserve of constitutional interpretation," which, as French doctrine indicates, is at the heart of the *pouvoir* of the constitutional court. It allows for a more creative reading of the constitution or—if the court so wills—a restrictive, passive decoding of its provisions, which in practice will mean abandoning the concept of building the so-called judicial constitution. If, however, the constitutional court decides to use interpretative reserves, it will act ambitiously and activistically, often supplementing and sometimes even changing the constitution by deriving from its textual layer norms, principles, and values not explicitly expressed *expressis verbis*.

A judicial constitution created under such conditions will significantly develop the actual text of the constitution, sometimes supplementing and modifying it, and in some cases even changing it. An example of this can be seen in the actions of the French Constitutional Council, which has often resorted to "interpretative reserves" (as the interpretation of laws in accordance with the constitution is referred to in France), effectively acting in favor of parliament by recognizing the constitutionality of a statutory norm examined in a preventive manner, provided that it is applied appropriately. This attitude of the Council led to it being referred to as a "specialized legislative chamber" (*chambre législative spécialisée*), which in its actions crosses the Rubicon of a constitutional court and effectively becomes a co-legislative body, and in some cases even a co-constitutional body[28] [24]. The constitutional reserve, or the interpretation of laws in accordance with the constitution, therefore leaves room for discretion on the part of the adjudicating body, which it may exercise depending on the circumstances, either by limiting its interpretation of the constitution or by giving it a creative, extensive form. Hence, constitutional reserves, as their French name suggests, allow the adjudicating body to decide on a case-by-case basis whether, and above all how serious and far-reaching, its interference in legislative activity developing the constitution should be. For example, the French Constitutional Council takes a cautious approach to them, assuming that excessive use of *réserves d'interprétation* may conflict with the freedom of political choices made by parliament, which also interprets the constitution, to which it is fully entitled, and which is reflected in the laws passed by parliament, which are an extension of the text of the constitution[29] [25, 26]. On the other hand, however, the use of reserves, even highly activist ones, may work to the advantage of parliament, as it allows it to avoid the extreme situation of having to repeal a provision[30] [27]. At the same time, as evidenced by the jurisprudence of the Constitutional Council, recourse to constitutional reserves is largely dependent on the constitutional matters within which the Council operates. Therefore, when the Council is to interfere in matters of rights and freedoms, it is more willing and more likely to use constitutional reservations. However, when the Council's case law does not involve determining the legal situation

[28] A. Stone Sweet, *Le Conseil constitutionnel et la transformation de la République*, „Cahiers du Conseil Constitutionnel" 2009, nr 25, p. 66.

[29] Décision n° 2010–2 QPC. The Constitutional Council draws on constitutional provisions in its rulings. See, e.g. Décision 84–181 DC; Décision n° 2002–463 DC; Décision n° 2024–1,089 QPC; Décision n° 2020–873 QPC; Décision n° 2018-730 QPC; Décision n° 2023–1,076 QPC; Décision n° 2021–934 QPC; Décision n° 2018–765 QPC; Décision n° 2019-799/800 QPC; Décision n° 2016–601 QPC. For more information on the judicial practice of constitutional interpretation, see: *Interpreting Constitutions. A Comparative Study*, ed. J. Goldsworthy, New York 2006, *passim*.

[30] O. Dord, *La QPC et le Parlement: une bienveillance réciproque*, „Les Nouveaux Cahiers du Conseil Constitutionnel" 2013, nr 38, p. 31.

of an individual, constitutional reservations remain outside the Council's decision-making scope, which means that the ordinary legislator has much greater freedom and the activity of the judicial body is much less visible[31] [28]. Nevertheless, the very concept of interpretative reservations, or the interpretation of laws in accordance with the constitution, proves the importance and seriousness of the interpretative activity of the constitutional court, which always, even when exercising self-restraint in its jurisprudence, decides on the interpretation of the constitution, either by expanding it and thus creating a so-called judicial constitution, or by confining it to the textual layer.

Of course, when discussing interpretations of the constitution, other forms of reading the text of the fundamental law should also be taken into account. Hence, incidentally, the concept of interpretation, which is not reserved for the courts, is so important[32] [23]. Judicial interpretation, and in particular interpretation by the constitutional court, is only one way of interpreting the constitution (although it is clear that it is of fundamental importance for this interpretation). Another is constitutional practice (together with the accompanying doctrine of constitutional law), which in some cases can go much further than judicial interpretation. There are plenty of examples showing that practice plays a significant role in the process of exegesis of textual constitutional norms. Suffice it to mention the American institution of judicial review, which, as we know, is a highly specific institution of American constitutionalism that is still absent from the text of the Constitution, yet one that has significantly corrected, if not revolutionized, that text. Another important change, revealed in over 200 years of practice in applying the US Constitution, is the emergence of the institution of presidential legislative leadership, in circumstances where the original text of the Constitution does not even grant the president the right of legislative initiative, while practice creates him as the authentic Chief Legislator. Another example of an equally ambitious constitutional practice, which was sufficiently autonomous from the text of the constitution that it essentially shaped a new state of constitutional regulation, was the French *la Constitution Grévy*, which effectively challenged some of the constitutional provisions, establishing alternative solutions in their place, which over time came to be recognized as the binding constitution, to such an extent that any violation of them was perceived as a constitutional offense. The Grévy Constitution invalidated certain classic solutions that were part of the canon of the parliamentary system (e.g., the presidential veto of a bill or the right of the head of state to dissolve parliament prematurely), while at the same time establishing *via facti* others that were a hyperbole of the relationship between the government and parliament (e.g., the obligation for the government to resign in the event of any defeat in a parliamentary vote, regardless of the importance of the matter, which was intended to express respect for the principles of the parliamentary system and, consequently, the obligation for the government to be supported by an arithmetic majority in

[31] For more on this topic, see: A. Viala, *Les réserves d'interprétation dans la jurisprudence du Conseil constitutionne*, Paris 1999, *passim*.

[32] Francis Delpérée points out that "In a democratic society, interpreting the Constitution is everyone's business. However, only interpretations made by public authorities can have legal effect. That is why it is this interpretation that attracts attention" ((in the original: "*L'interprétation de la Constitution est, dans une société démocratique, l'affaire de tous. Seule pourtant l'interprétation qui émane d'autorités publiques est susceptible de produire des effets juridiques. C'est donc elle qui retient exclusivement l'attention*") – Por. F. Delpérée, *La Constitution et son interpretation . . .*, p. 187.

parliament). The interpretation, or rather reinterpretation, of the Constitution, this time of the Fifth Republic, was also cohabitation, which, as has been rightly pointed out, constituted the most significant change to the existing Constitution of 1958. It established a solution previously absent from the Fifth Republic's system, namely the principle of political and party diversity in the institutional triangle of head of state, government, and parliament, which caused the entire concept of semi-presidentialism *à la française* to begin to erode, and France slowly transformed into a parliamentary system. The phenomenon of cohabitation was not so much, as is sometimes perceived, a matter of the different political and party backgrounds of the bodies that made up the system of government, but rather a change in constitutional relations within them caused by the political and party arrangement. As a result, the strong presidential profile of the system was weakened, as the relationship between the government and parliament, typical of a parliamentary system, took precedence, pushing the president into the shadows of the system of government. This fact is often overlooked, and the term cohabitation is used to describe any situation in which the head of state and the government come from different political backgrounds (camps), regardless of the consequences of this fact for the political system. Meanwhile, the essence of cohabitation and the fact that it actually reinterpreted the constitutional relations between state bodies was that this separation triggered institutional reconstruction, while at the same time determining the flexibility of the Fifth Republic, which in moments of political convergence is more presidential in nature, while in moments of cohabitation it becomes more parliamentary.

5. Conclusion(s)

Interpretation is the search for the meaning of words and phrases, the meaning of the will expressed by the author of a legal norm, a meaning that often emerges from several scattered provisions[33] [33, 9]. In this case, it is irrelevant whether such research is neutral or unconsciously conveys elements of a subjective nature, whether it is conducted in an adequate manner or omits certain possibilities of legal reasoning, and whether it remains outside the scope of legislative action or participates in its own way in the process of law-making. In reality, what matters is only the approach of the entity interpreting the meaning of thoughts, symbols, and meanings encoded in the text of the constitution. The result of the interpretation is to determine the exact meaning of legal norms, which is all the more important in the case of the constitution, since the constitution – by definition – is a highly vague, broad act that affects the entire legal system.

Interpretation is also explanation. It is the collection of terms, concepts, and meanings that can explain what is unclear or ambiguous in the text of the constitution. Interpretation also involves revealing the cause or consequences of a provision whose meaning may not be prima facie obvious. Nevertheless, the difference between "mere" commentary and interpretation is crucial. Interpretation is about clarifying how the meaning of the constitution and its subordinate legal acts should be understood. Furthermore, interpretation must never depart from the text, the letter, or the spirit of the constitution. Therefore, Henri Batiffol points out that when accepting

[33] M. Troper, *Constitutional Interpretation...*, p. 37.

a constitution, it is always about "concern for truth" but also about "concern for loyalty"[34] [29] in order to remain faithful to the constitution, not only in terms of its letter but also the entire layer not written *expressis verbis*, that is, the historical, functional, teleological, and axiological approach. The most important duty in the process of interpreting the constitution is always loyalty to the constitution. This means that any technique used to explain the meaning of constitutional norms cannot be unconstitutional. Differences between methods of interpretation cease to be significant if they are not guided by a fundamental directive, that is, the directive of pro-constitutional interpretation. It should be the guiding principle for every type of inquiry and every interpretative technique. Unlike interpretation, commentary, which is reserved for constitutional law doctrine, can do much more. It does not have to adhere strictly to orthodoxy; it can be more comprehensive, it can interpret the meaning of constitutional concepts and meanings more creatively, it can formulate various postulates or even alternative ways of interpreting the constitution. It can also propose various "new approaches" or "new paradigms," which remain academic proposals, albeit sometimes interesting, original, and worthy of attention.

One of such proposals is the so-called evolutionary (dynamic) interpretation, which is increasingly popular in the doctrine of constitutional law. It is suspended between the need to adapt the constitution to the conditions in which it applies and the temptation of an instrumental approach to the law, which, in extreme cases, may even turn out to be unconstitutional. For these reasons, evolutionary interpretation should, at most, remain within the bounds of commentary, which is much freer and therefore much less binding. However, it should be very cautious when it moves to the position of interpretation. This is all the more true when we realize that "to interpret is also to agree"[35] [9] (*interpréter, c'est encore accorder*). The process of interpreting a constitution is, after all, nothing more than a search for possible reconciliations between the necessarily vague, general, and perhaps outdated text of the constitution and a precise, specific situation that requires constitutional adequacy for it to maintain its legitimacy [36] [30]. Nevertheless, no interpretation, especially when carried out by a judge, can be abstract and purely conceptual, conducted in isolation from the text, even if it is old and outdated. A constitution, whatever its form, establishes a boundary, which means that if one wishes to cross it, a new constitution must be enacted, and interpretation does not imply arbitrary application of the constitution.

Hence, the process of constitutional interpretation should be subject to certain minimum conditions. First and foremost, regardless of the interpretive technique used, the model for interpreting the meaning of the constitution should always be a pro-constitutional interpretation. Second, the interpreting entity cannot ignore historical interpretation or, in the circumstances of the US Constitution, so-called originalism, meaning the closest approximation of the meaning of the constitution to its original meaning[37] [31]. This means, in other words, that the assumption is that interpretation is an act of cognition, not an act of will, which inevitably imposes certain limitations on deriving entirely new, let alone unfamiliar, content from

---

[34] H. Batiffol, *Questions de l'interprétation juridique*, "Archives de Philosophie de Droit", 1972, tome XVII, p. 18.

[35] M. Troper, *Constitutional Interpretation...*, p. 38.

[36] M. Coutu, *Légitimité et Constitution: les trois types purs de la jurisprudence constitutionnelle*, "Droit et Société" 2004, no 56–57, pp. 233–257.

[37] For more on originalism and the application of this method in US practice, see: *Interpreting the Constitution: the debate over original intent,* ed, J.N. Rakove, Boston 1990, *passim.*

a constitution. Third, as always, originalism cannot be an absolute and unconditional principle. Interpretation, especially when applied to older constitutions created in diametrically opposed historical, social, political, and even economic circumstances, must take into account the praxeological purpose of every interpretation, and this is the adaptation of the constitution to contemporary conditions. The constitution, however, is not an antiquarian prop but the fundamental law upon which the entire current legal order rests. This necessarily leads to a transformation of the constitution[38] [32–34], which, however, is not unlimited but should be cautious, rational, and balanced, which all the more suggests treating the constitution as a compromise, for example, between regionalism and the requirement for constitutional transformation. Fourth, and finally, the framework for interpretation is most often defined, to some extent, by the constitution itself. It creates a catalog of principles and values, and these define an axiological system, which is established, among other things, to generate boundary conditions for future interpretation. Any reading of the constitution must remain coherent with the values contained therein, although this does not mean that the interpreter cannot prioritize these values or assign them new meanings, which is also a consequence of interpretation.

[38] For more on this topic, see: J.P. Langa, *Transformative constitutionalism*, "Stellenbosch Law Review" 2006, no 17, pp. 351–360; M. Hailbronner, *Transformative constitutionalism: Not only in the global south*, "The American Journal of Comparative Law" 2017, no 3, pp. 527–565; and K.E. Klare, *Legal culture and transformative constitutionalism*, "South African Journal on Human Rights" 1998, no 1, pp.146–188.

Author details

Jarosław Szymanek
Academy of Justice, Warsaw, Poland

*Address all correspondence to: jaroslaw.szymanek@aws.edu.pl

References

[1] Frydman B. Le Sens Des Lois: Histoire de L'interprétation Et de la Raison Juridique. Paris; 2011

[2] Troper M. L'interprétation constitutionnelle. In: Mélin-Soucramanien F, ed. L'interprétation Constitutionnelle. Paris; 2005. p. 13–25

[3] Derrida J. Law, Justice and Interpretation. New York; 2006

[4] Bourdieu P, and Wacquant L. La force du droit: éléments pour une sociologie du champ juridique. Actes de la Recherche En Sciecnes Sociales. 1986;**64**:3–19

[5] Dupret B.Droit et sciences sociales. Pour une respécification praxéologique. Droit Et Société. 2010;n° **75**(2):315–335

[6] Legendre P. L'amour du Conseur. Essai Sur L'orde Dogmatique. Paris; 1974

[7] Aguila Y. Cinq questions sur l'interpretation constitutionnelle. Revue Francaise de Droit Constitutionell. 1995;**21**:9–46

[8] Wheare KC. Modern Constitutions. London – New York – Toronto; 1967

[9] Troper M. Constitutional Interpretation. Israel Law Review. 2006;**39**(2):35–50

[10] Delnoy P. Elements de méthodologie juridique: Méthodologie de l'interprétation juridique. Méthodologie de L'application du Droit, Liège. 2005

[11] Sarkowicz K. Uwagi o współczesnej interpretacji prawniczej. In: Wronkowska S, ed. Polska Kultura Prawna a Proces Integracji Europejskiej. 2005. p. 11–30

[12] Kaleta KJ. Wykładnia prawa jako forma włączy politycznej. Stanowiska wobec interpretacji konstytucji w doktrynie francuskiej. In: Stawecki T, Winczorek J, eds. Wykładnia Konstytucji. Warszawa: Inspiracje, Teorie, Argumenty; 2014. p. 57–79

[13] Carbonnier J. Droit Civil. Paris: 2004. p. 57–79

[14] Troper M. Le problème de l'interprétation et la théorie de la supralégalité constitutionnel. In: Recueil D'étude En Hommage Charles Eisenmann. Paris; 1975. p. 133–151

[15] Goyard-Fabre S. Les Principes Philospohique du Droit Politique Moderne. Paris: 1997

[16] Jan P. Le Procès Constitutionnel. Paris: 2010

[17] Guiselin E-P. Le Droit de la Vie Politique. Paris: 2004

[18] Chevallier J. Droit Et Politique. Paris: 1993

[19] Rousseau D. Question de constitution. In: Colliard J-C, Jegouzo Y, eds. Le Nouveau Constitutionnalisme. Mélanges En L'honneur de Gérard Conac. Paris; 2001. p. 3–30

[20] Poimeur Y, Rosenberg D. La doctrine constitutionnelle et le constitutionnalisme français. In: Lochak D, ed. Les Usages Sociaux du Droit. Paris; 1989. p. 230–251

[21] Troper M. La liberté d'interprétation du juge constitutionnel. In: Amselek P, ed. Interprétation de Drot. Bruxelles; 1995. p. 223–245

[22] Langlois R. L'application des règles d'interprétation constitutionnelle. Les Cahiers de Droit. 1987;28(**1**):207–221

[23] Delpérée F. La Constitution et son interprétation. In: Van de Kerchove M, Gérard P, eds. L' Interpretation En Droit. Approche Pluridisciplinaire. Bruxelles; 1978. p. 187–210

[24] Stone Sweet A. Le Conseil constitutionnel et la transformation de la République. Cahiers du Conseil Constitutionnel. 2009;**25**:65–69

[25] Goldsworthy J, ed. Interpreting Constitutions: A Comparative Study. Oxford: Oxford University Press; 2006

[26] Interpreting Constitutions. A Comparative Study. Goldsworthy J, ed., New York: 2006

[27] Dord O. La QPC et le Parlement: Une bienveillance réciproque. Les Nouveaux Cahiers du Conseil Constitutionnel. 2013;N° **38**(1):23–36.

[28] Viala A. Les Réserves D'interprétation Dans la Jurisprudence du Conseil Constitutionne. Paris; 1999

[29] Batiffol H. *Questions de L'interprétation Juridique*, Archives de Philosophie de Droit. 1972, tome XVII

[30] Coutu M. Légitimité et Constitution: Les trois types purs de la jurisprudence constitutionnelle. Droit Et Société. 2004;**56–57**:233–257

[31] Rakove JN. Interpreting the Constitution: The Debate over Original Intent. Boston; 1990

[32] Langa JP. Transformative constitutionalism. Stellenbosch Law Review. 2006;17:351–360

[33] Hailbronner M. Transformative constitutionalism: Not only in the global south. The American Journal of Comparative Law. 2017;**65**(3):527–565

[34] Klare KE. Legal culture and transformative constitutionalism. South African Journal on Human Rights. 1998;**14**(1):146–188

Chapter 5

Perspective Chapter: New Tendencies in Post-Communist Constitutionalism–The Case of Central and Eastern Europe

Jacek Wojnicki

Abstract

This chapter discusses new trends in the constitutionalism of post-communist countries located in Central and Eastern Europe. The political-systemic analysis covers six countries that underwent profound systemic transformation after 1989: Poland, Hungary, the Czech Republic, Slovakia, Romania, and Bulgaria. These nations moved away, albeit at different speeds, from the model of a socialist state, a shift that was reflected in several key developments: (1) the loss of political power by communist parties; (2) the inclusion of opposition groups in legal, social, and political life (political pluralism); (3) the holding of competitive elections for legislative bodies and local self-government councils; and (4) the process of constitutional change. This last political trend unfolded in several distinct stages. The analysis also considers the practical application of constitutional regulations in political life, as this provides the clearest indication of how a democratic system operates within a given state. The main research question centres on whether it is possible to identify common features in the constitutional processes of Central and Eastern European countries after 1989. A secondary question asks what new trends can be observed in the constitutionalism of the post-communist countries in the region. The analysis employs several research methods characteristic of political science, including historical-descriptive analysis, legal-institutional analysis, the comparative method, and the decision-making method.

Keywords: constitutionalism, democratisation, transformation, system of government, post-communism, political pluralism, rule of law

1. Introduction

This chapter discusses new trends in the constitutionalism of post-communist countries located in Central and Eastern Europe. The political-systemic analysis covers six countries that underwent profound systemic transformation after 1989: Poland, Hungary, the Czech Republic, Slovakia, Romania, and Bulgaria. These nations moved away, albeit at different speeds, from the model of a socialist state, a shift that was reflected in several key developments: (1) the loss of political power by communist parties, (2) the inclusion of opposition groups in legal social and political life (political pluralism), (3) the holding of competitive elections for legislative bodies and local self-government councils, and (4) the process of constitutional change. This last political trend unfolded in several distinct stages [1–3]. The analysis also considers the practical application of constitutional regulations in political life, as this provides the clearest indication of how a democratic system operates within a given state. The main research question centres on whether it is possible to identify common features in the constitutional processes of Central and Eastern European countries after 1989. A secondary question asks what new trends can be observed in the constitutionalism of the post-communist countries in the region. The analysis employs several research methods characteristic of political science, including historical-descriptive analysis, legal-institutional analysis, the comparative method, and the decision-making method.

2. The first stage of systemic transformation

Systemic transformations marked a fundamental stage in the broader political changes initiated in the countries of this region [4–7]. One of the key effects of these socio-political changes was the inclusion of opposition groups in social and political life. Historical parties (a term used in reference to political parties that had operated legally before the communist era) were legalised, alongside newly formed umbrella-type opposition movements. These included Poland's Solidarity, which functioned not only as a typical trade union but also as a broad socio-political movement, the Czech-based Civic Forum, Slovakia's Public Against Violence, and Bulgaria's Union of Democratic Forces (UDF). At the same time, new political parties began to emerge, without direct predecessors in the pre-communist period, such as liberal and environmental factions. Transforming the constitutional order that had functioned in the socialist state was a precondition for democratic reform – a goal explicitly stated by most of the political elite. The following countries were officially defined as socialist states in their constitutional texts: Poland from 1976, Czechoslovakia from 1960, Hungary from 1972, Romania from 1965, and Bulgaria from 1971 [8]. Relevant provisions were found in a dedicated chapter of the constitution outlining the state's socio-political system. Hence, the first stage of constitutional change involved amendments aimed at de-ideologising constitutional regulations; examples include constitutional revisions in Czechoslovakia on 29 November 1989, Bulgaria on 15 January 1990, and, though not discussed in this analysis, the German Democratic Republic on 1 December 1989. These amendments removed references to the leading role of the communist party and the friendship with the Union of Soviet Socialist Republics and other socialist states. They also eliminated provisions defining the state according to the principles of communist ideology, including those that identified the working people of town and country, rather than the nation itself, as the sovereign entity [9, 10].

The process of constitutional change unfolded differently in Poland and Hungary. Over the course of 1989, the progress of pro-democratic reforms, initiated by segments of the ruling elites, allowed for a constitutional compromise to be reached between the government and parts of the opposition in both countries. As a result, new political institutions were introduced in Poland (the April 1989 amendment: the establishment of the presidency, a second chamber of parliament, and the National Council of the Judiciary) and in Hungary (the October 1989 amendment: the establishment of the presidency and parliamentary ombudsmen, the restoration of local self-government, and the reinstatement of the traditional structure and name of the armed forces). Under the December 1989 amendment – adopted during the term of the first non-communist prime minister in the region, the Catholic activist and Solidarity adviser Tadeusz Mazowiecki – Poland's constitution was further revised to demythologise it by renaming the state as the Republic of Poland, restoring the traditional state emblem, and removing references to the leading role of the communist party and the alliance with the USSR. Another key aspect of this amendment was the reintroduction of provisions concerning the socio-economic system within the context of a market economy. These included the freedom of economic activity and the principle of legal equality between the three main forms of ownership: private, cooperative, and state. In Hungary, the October 1989 amendment introduced the aforementioned changes, removing the ideological foundations of the constitutional law that had been in force prior to 1989 [7].

Romania experienced a different constitutional situation. As a result of the quasi-revolutionary changes of December 1989, which saw the violent overthrow of the dictatorship led by Nicolae Ceaușescu's clan, a decision was made to reject the existing political order, including the 1965 Constitution of the Socialist Republic of Romania. Therefore, new constitutional regulations were decreed by the National Salvation Front, the interim governing body established after 22 December 1989 and from 1 February 1990, by the Provisional Council of National Unity, which included representatives of historical factions. A key constitutional-level document from this period was the decree-law of 14 March 1990 on parliamentary and presidential elections. This act went beyond the function of a standard electoral law; in practice, it served as a provisional constitutional law that determined the structure of both parliament and the head of state, introducing a bicameral legislature (the Chamber of Deputies and the Senate) and retaining the office of the president, which had originally been established under the communist regime in the spring of 1974 [11].

3. Further stages of constitutional transformation

The next stage of constitutional change in Central and Eastern Europe involved the process of drafting and adopting new constitutional acts to mark the culmination of democratisation efforts and to lay the foundation for the new socio-political order within the state [12, 13]. At this point in the analysis, it is also important to highlight another key aspect: the emergence of new state entities following the dissolution of three socialist federations – Yugoslavia, the USSR, and Czechoslovakia. This chapter offers a more detailed analysis of the case of Czechoslovakia and the subsequent emergence, in January 1993, of two independent states – the Czech Republic and the Slovak Republic – as a result of its dissolution. However, attention should also be given to the Yugoslav and Soviet republics, which became new, independent states in 1992, often without an established tradition of statehood, as in the cases of Bosnia and Herzegovina, Macedonia, and Belarus. In these countries, the formation of a stable state structure became the primary objective, while democratic and market reforms were relegated to the background, with all the resulting consequences for political, social, and economic life. Accordingly, the first constitutions were adopted in two post-Yugoslav republics, which were still formally part of the SFRY at the time: the Republic of Serbia (September 1990) and the Republic of Croatia (December 1990). The Serbian case is particularly noteworthy, as the constitution was drafted and adopted by a parliament elected back in 1986, still dominated by the post-communist Socialist Party of Serbia. However, a referendum was held to approve the constitution, introducing an element of democratic procedure to the country's socio-political system [14].

Constitution-makers in Central Europe faced the formidable task of laying solid foundations for a stable democratic system. In a fundamental systemic shift, they abandoned the principle of the unity of state power and introduced (or restored) the principle of the separation and balance of powers [12]. In shaping new constitutional arrangements, they drew on diverse sources of inspiration: (1) negation – by rejecting the constitutional principles of real socialism; (2) continuation – by drawing on domestic traditions from before the communist period and elements of the democratic strand of socialist constitutionalism; (3) reception – by borrowing from Western European constitutionalism, particularly in the areas of civil rights and liberties and systems of government [15]. Tadeusz Mołdawa [12], a Polish constitution-maker and scholar of Central European political systems, emphasised that the reception of Western solutions provided the foundations for the rule of law, political pluralism, and democratic and effective governance. Maria Kruk [16], a Polish constitutional law scholar, noted that the general catalogue of principles embedded in the Polish (and not only Polish) post-1989 constitutional act included the following elements: democracy and pluralism, human rights, a democratic system of government, the effectiveness and stability of democratic rule, fair and democratic law, a market economy with a social dimension, Polish traditions, and European standards.

An important aspect of political transformation in Central and Eastern Europe was the restoration (in some countries, the *de facto* introduction) of political pluralism as a key feature of the democratic state. Reflecting this trend, Central and Eastern European countries held competitive elections, although not all of them met the criteria of free and democratic parliamentary contests. In several countries, heads of state were also elected by popular vote, either in collegial form (as in the cases of Slovenia and Bosnia) or monocratic form as the office of the president (as in the cases of Romania, Serbia, Ukraine, and Russia). However, it should be noted that not all of these elections resulted in an alternation of power and the removal of communist or post-communist politicians from office [17, 18]. The first case of alternation of power occurred in Poland, where the government of Tadeusz Mazowiecki was formed in September 1989, even though the parliamentary elections held on 4 and 18 June 1989 did not meet all the criteria of a free and democratic vote, particularly due to the so-called contract agreement governing the composition of the lower chamber, the Sejm. Under that arrangement, 65% of the seats (299 mandates) were allocated to the existing ruling coalition, while representatives of the social side, primarily the Solidarity Civic Committee centred around Lech Wałęsa, were permitted to contest the remaining 35% (161 seats). The second country to see an alternation of power was Czechoslovakia, where a new government with the participation of representatives of Civic Forum and Public Against Violence was formed on 10 December 1989. On 29 December 1989, the parliament, still dominated by the communist party, elected Václav Havel, the leader of the so-called Velvet Revolution, as president of the republic. The third country to witness an alternation of power was Hungary, where a coalition government led by the Christian Democrat politician József Antall was formed in May 1990, following the first free elections to the National Assembly. In the remaining countries, the first competitive elections confirmed the stable position of post-communist parties and the relative weakness of democratic forces, as seen in Romania, Serbia, Belarus, and Ukraine. Bulgaria was a special case: its socialist party, the successor to the communist party, scored a landslide victory in the parliamentary elections in June 1990, but as a result of a political stalemate, the candidate of the UDF, Zhelyu Zhelev, was elected president on 1 August 1990 [4, 19, 20].

Paradoxically, the countries that led the way in systemic transformation were not the first to adopt new constitutional acts. Maria Kruk concluded: 'Other post-socialist states of Central and Eastern Europe formally carried out this transformation earlier, if we measure this process by the adoption of new constitutions. However, this does not mean that they had actually completed their transformation any earlier.' [16]. As already mentioned, in both Poland and Hungary, a preliminary outline of a constitutional compromise between the communist elites and opposition politicians had been reached as early as 1989. This included the most essential features of a democratic system: the democratic rule of law, constitutional supremacy, the separation and balance of powers, political pluralism, the decentralisation of public authority, a broad catalogue of rights and freedoms, and the foundations of a socio-economic system based on a market (capitalist) economy. For this reason, most political elites, from both the post-communist camp and the mainstream opposition, viewed this framework as a sufficiently solid foundation for a democratic form of government. Consequently, they chose to focus on immediate socio-economic reforms [1, 12]. The plans to adopt new constitutions were pushed into the background. In the Polish case, the key limiting factor was the non-representative nature of the parliament elected in June 1989, which, for obvious reasons, could not act as a constituent assembly. In designing new systems of government, constitution-makers in the region usually drew inspiration from Germany's Basic Law of May 1949 and the Constitution of the French Fifth Republic of September 1958. Notably, both constitutions established stable and effective executive authorities. In Germany, power was centred on the federal government and its chancellor; in France, both branches of the executive – the President of the Republic and the government – were strengthened. Legal experts and politicians in Warsaw, Budapest, Prague, and Ljubljana closely followed the chancellor model, while those in Bucharest, Zagreb, and Belgrade sought to replicate the French solutions. At this point, it is worth citing the conclusion of the Polish constitutional scholar Wojciech Sokolewicz, who emphasised: 'Every constitution should be tailored to the social context in which it is to function; it should reflect the actual social relations and social consciousness of the time, and it must take into account the historical traditions of the nation.' [21].

This is why new constitutions were first adopted in two Balkan states, Bulgaria and Romania, where the constituent assemblies were dominated by post-communist parties. This outcome may appear paradoxical only at first glance. In fact, post-communist politicians were eager to demonstrate their commitment to democratic and pro-market principles by adopting new constitutions. These constitutional acts were thus intended to serve as symbolic 'calling cards' of the new democracies in Central and Eastern Europe, as described by the Polish constitutional scholar

Stanisław Gebethner [22]. The Bulgarian constitution, the first such act among the discussed post-communist countries, was adopted at a session of the Grand National Assembly on 11 July 1991 [23, 24]. In Romania, the constitution was adopted at a joint session of both chambers of parliament on 21 November 1991, although, in this case, a decision was made to hold a referendum to approve the text [23, 25].

In the case of Czechoslovakia, no new constitution was adopted after 1989 due to growing disagreements between Czech and Slovak politicians, which ultimately led to the decision to dissolve the federal state at the end of 1992 [26]. In this situation, both republican parliaments – the Czech National Council and the Slovak National Council, elected in June 1992 – began drafting separate constitutions for the Czech Republic and the Slovak Republic. The latter was adopted first, at a session held on 1 September 1992. It was the second constitution of an independent Slovak state, following that of the Slovak Republic, which existed between 1939 and 1945. The new Slovak constitution drew on Western European constitutional traditions – including republican values, the democratic rule of law, the separation of powers and political pluralism – and, to some extent, on Czechoslovak constitutionalism, particularly that of the First Republic. However, the stance taken by most Slovak politicians towards the legacy of the common Czechoslovak state placed the new republic in a more difficult position: it could not directly refer to Czechoslovak legal solutions or claim continuity with Czechoslovak statehood. By contrast, the Czech approach was comparatively straightforward. Czech lawmakers chose to directly adopt many legal and constitutional solutions from Czechoslovakia. For example, they incorporated the Charter of Fundamental Rights and Freedoms of January 1991 into the Czech constitutional order. They also adopted a number of symbolic elements intended to link the new Czech state with the international legacy of Czechoslovakia: they retained the national holiday of 28 October (the anniversary of the founding of Czechoslovakia in 1918), adopted a flag and coat of arms with similar design and colours and elected the last president of Czechoslovakia, Václav Havel, as the first president of the Czech Republic, making him the head of state of two countries (he served four incomplete terms). It is also worth noting that the Czech National Council adopted the constitution of the new Czech state at a session held on 16 December 1992. Unlike the Slovak constitutional act, it referred explicitly both to the doctrine of Czechoslovak constitutionalism, particularly that of the First Republic, and to specific institutional arrangements, such as the structure of government and the procedure for its formation, the procedure for electing the President of the Republic, and the structure of the judiciary [27, 28].

It is worth considering how the constitution-makers defined the state. According to Article 1 of the Bulgarian Constitution, the Republic of Bulgaria is a 'parliamentary republic'. 'All state power derives from the people. It is exercised by the people directly and through the bodies provided for in this Constitution'. The Constitution of the Czech Republic defines it as 'a sovereign, unitary and democratic state founded on respect for the rights and freedoms of the individual and citizen' (Article 1). The Polish Constitution describes the Republic of Poland as 'the common good of all its citizens'. It is 'a democratic state governed by the rule of law, implementing the principles of social justice'. It is also defined as a unitary state (Articles 1–3). A more detailed definition appears in the 1991 Romanian Constitution. The constitution-makers defined Romania as 'a sovereign and independent, unitary and indivisible national state'. 'The form of government of the Romanian state is the republic. Romania is a democratic and social state governed by the rule of law, in which human dignity, citizens' rights and freedoms, the free development of personality, justice and political pluralism represent supreme values, in the spirit of the democratic traditions of the Romanian people and of the Revolution of 1989, and are constitutionally guaranteed' (Article 1). According to Article 1 of the Slovak Constitution, the Slovak Republic is 'a sovereign, democratic state governed by the rule of law. It is not linked to any ideology or religion'. In 1989, Hungarian constitution-makers declared that 'the Republic of Hungary is an independent, democratic state governed by the rule of law'. 'In the Republic of Hungary, all power belongs to the people, who exercise their sovereign rights through their elected representatives and directly. No activity of any social organisation, state body or citizen may be aimed at seizing or exercising power by force, nor at holding it exclusively. Everyone has the right and duty to resist such efforts in a lawful manner' (Article 1 of the 1989 Hungarian Constitution) [29]. These definitions of the state clearly refer to the contemporary constitutionalism of Western Europe, particularly the German Basic Law of May 1949, with its concept of the democratic and social state governed by the rule of law. In Romania, due to its cultural and linguistic ties with France, there are visible references to French constitutionalism, especially the Constitution of September 1958 that established the Fifth Republic. In this context, it is worth noting that in the early 1990s, French scholars and constitutional lawyers participated in the legislative work of Romania's Chamber of Deputies and Senate at the invitation of the government in Bucharest.

Implementing key institutions into the constitutional practice of the new democratic states in Central and Eastern Europe proved to be a drawn-out process. The new constitutional regulations introduced important institutions aimed at safeguarding the rule of law and ensuring respect for citizens' rights and freedoms. In this context, one notable example is the establishment of ombudsman institutions in the post-communist countries [30]. Poland was the first to introduce such an office; this took place in July 1987, during the final phase of the People's Republic (PRL [Polska Rzeczpospolita Ludowa]) [22]. The next country to incorporate the institution of the ombudsman into its constitutional order was the Republic of Hungary. In October 1989, it adopted a major constitutional amendment that provided for two ombudsmen: one for civil and human rights and another for the rights of national and ethnic minorities [31]. However, the first parliamentary ombudsmen were not appointed by the National Assembly until 1995. In two Balkan countries, the decision to establish ombudsman institutions (in Romania, it was called the People's Advocate) was made in the first constitutional acts adopted in 1991. However, introducing these bodies into constitutional practice took a long time: in Romania, this occurred only in March 1997, and in Bulgaria – in January 2004. This delay illustrates the sensitivity surrounding the protection of human and civil rights and the lack of understanding of its essence among the political elites of both countries. Similarly, in both countries formed following the break-up of Czechoslovakia, the establishment of ombudsman institutions took several years. In the Czech Republic, the office was created in 2000; in the neighbouring Slovak Republic – in February 2002. In the former, the key factor was opposition from the country's long-serving prime minister, Václav Klaus, who argued that establishing an ombudsman implied distrust in the independence of the judiciary. In Slovakia, which until September 1998 struggled with the undemocratic exercise of power by the Mečiar camp, calls for creating an ombudsman came from democratic and liberal opposition parties opposed to the ruling HZDS.

Establishing the institution became possible only after the alternation of power and the removal of the Mečiar camp from office following the formation of the Slovak Democratic Coalition in July 1997 and its success in the September 1998 elections to the National Council of the Slovak Republic [32].

A key feature of a democratic state governed by the rule of law – as all the discussed Central and Eastern European countries have defined themselves since the early 1990s – is the guarantee of legality and the rule of law. This constitutional doctrine led to the establishment of constitutional courts. Czechoslovakia, the predecessor of both the Czech Republic and the Slovak Republic, was among the first countries to introduce such a court under a constitutional act adopted in February 1920, based on the doctrine of the Austrian jurist Hans Kelsen. Consequently, it was the only Central European country that, in the pre-communist period, had both the practice and institutional experience of constitutional review carried out by a body created specifically for that purpose. It is also worth noting that the constitutional law of October 1968, which established the Czechoslovak federation, formally provided for the creation of a constitutional court. However, no legislative steps were taken to this effect until the Velvet Revolution of November 1989. The Constitutional Court of Czechoslovakia was not established until 1991 and operated for just over 20 months, until the dissolution of the federal state. Both successor states, the Czech Republic and the Slovak Republic, solemnly declared the establishment of constitutional courts in their new constitutions, drawing directly on the Czechoslovak legacy in this area. The Constitutional Court of the Czech Republic was established in July 1993, and the Constitutional Court of the Slovak Republic in March 1993. It is also noteworthy that both countries chose their second-largest cities – Brno and Košice, respectively – as the location of these courts as part of an effort to deconcentrate key state institutions [33, 34].

In the period of the Second Republic, Polish constitutional law did not include the institution of constitutional review, as it was considered incompatible with the principle of parliamentary sovereignty [35]. A similar approach was taken after the Second World War, when the political system of the People's Republic of Poland was being formed, drawing heavily on the Stalinist Constitution of 1936. The first signs of academic interest in the constitutionality of law emerged in the mid-1970s. The issue entered the public debate during the period of heightened political engagement in 1980–1981, when Solidarity operated legally, not only as a trade union movement but also as a broad socio-political force that expressed social aspirations and demands. The demand to create a Constitutional Tribunal, alongside a restored State Tribunal, appeared among the programme resolutions of the twelfth Congress of the Democratic Party, then a legal political organisation representing the intelligentsia and artisans. Parliamentary work on amending the constitution began in the autumn of 1981 and was not suspended even after martial law was imposed in December of that year. This continuity was intended to signal goodwill on the part of the government and to demonstrate that not all demands for democratising the PRL system had been rejected. The constitutional amendment was adopted in March 1982, followed by a detailed statute in April 1985. Poland thus became the second socialist country, after Yugoslavia, to establish a constitutional court [36, 37].

In Hungary, the constitutional court was introduced into the legal order through an amendment adopted in October 1989, negotiated during the so-called Round Table Talks between representatives of the government, legal socio-political organisations and opposition groups. The Constitutional Court began its operations in January 1990. In the two previously mentioned Balkan states, the establishment of constitutional courts took longer. In Romania, such a court, created under the November 1991 constitution, began functioning in June 1992. The longest delay in implementing a constitutional review mechanism occurred in the Republic of Bulgaria, where a constitutional court was not established until October 1997, following the democratic alternation of power in June 1997 [30, 38].

At this point in the analysis, it is important to emphasise that both the rule of law and the institutionalisation of mechanisms to guarantee the protection of human and civil rights, particularly in the form of the ombudsman, serve as a kind of litmus test for the actual functioning of a democratic system. It is therefore neither surprising nor unexpected that introducing both institutions into the constitutional order proved challenging in countries with only limited prior experience in this area, especially during the pre-communist period or the liberalisation of the socialist system in the 1980s [12].

4. Changes in the new constitutions

The next stage in the development of constitutionalism in the discussed countries involved amendments to the existing constitutional acts. These revisions stemmed from a range of factors: (1) the experience of undemocratic rule under Vladimír Mečiar in Slovakia (1992–1998), including the instrumental use of democratic political institutions or attempts to bypass them altogether – for example, the fourteen-month vacancy in the presidency; (2) the process of European integration and accession to the European Union (EU). In this context, the most detailed constitutional amendments were adopted in Bulgaria in 2007 and in Romania in 2003 [39–41]. In Poland, changes of this kind were more limited, involving the introduction of the European Arrest Warrant. Most amendments concerned the judiciary, fair trial safeguards, judicial independence, and the rights of national and ethnic minorities. In Slovakia, following the rise to power of a broad anti-Mečiar coalition, the constitutional act was amended twice, in 1999 and in 2001. The first amendment changed the procedure for electing the head of state by introducing direct presidential elections, although the office's powers and prerogatives remained unchanged. This was a direct response to the obstruction tactics used by the Mečiar camp between March and October 1998, which had prevented the election of a new head of state. In that situation, presidential powers were exercised by the government and its head – Mečiar himself. The 2001 constitutional changes were significantly broader in scope, addressing the relationship between the legislature and the executive as well as the balance of power between the government and the president [42, 43].

In Hungary, constitutional amendments up to 2010 applied to the version of the constitutional law adopted in August 1990, following the substantial revision of Act XX of August 1949. The most significant constitutional change concerned the procedure for electing the President of the Republic. This issue became a major point of contention with the communist side – which hoped to capitalise on the popularity of its potential candidate for the office, Imre Pozsgay, in the autumn of 1989 – but also caused friction among the main democratic political parties, including the liberals, Christian democrats, social democrats, and agrarians. Ultimately, in

May 1990, a decision was taken to introduce indirect election of the head of state by the National Assembly. This arrangement remains in force in Hungary to this day [29, 44].

The most stable constitutional regulations in force can be found in the Czech Republic, representing a positive example of respect for the idea of constitutionalism and the applicable law. It is worth noting that this reflects a continuation of constitutional practice originating from the First Republic. The only significant constitutional amendment was adopted in March 2012 and concerned the procedure for electing the president, replacing indirect elections – the model used in both Czechoslovakia and the Czech Republic after 1992 – with direct elections. At the same time, it should be emphasised that no changes have been made to the institutional position or role of the head of state within the structure of the highest state authorities [33].

5. Adoption of a new constitution

This case applies solely to the Republic of Hungary. In April 2010, an alternation of power occurred following parliamentary elections, with the FIDESZ camp assuming control. The party, in coalition with the Christian Democrats (KDNP), secured a constitutional majority, which made it possible to draft and adopt a new constitution for the Hungarian state. This aligned perfectly with the official narrative of Viktor Orbán's camp, which condemned the post-communist period and declared the dawn of a new socio-political and constitutional era. In this context, the new Fundamental Law became a manifesto of the new government and its transformed vision of the state [45, 46]. Particularly noteworthy is the elaborate and thorough definition of the national and state community contained in the section titled Foundations: 'The name of our HOMELAND is Hungary. Hungary is an independent, democratic state governed by the rule of law. The Hungarian state's form of government is a republic. The source of public power is the people. The people exercise their power through elected representatives or, in exceptional cases, in a direct manner. The functioning of the Hungarian state is based on the principle of the separation of powers. No person's activity may be aimed at the forcible acquisition or exercise of power, nor at its exclusive possession. Everyone has the right and obligation to resist such attempts in a lawful way. The state is authorised to use coercion in order to enforce the Fundamental Law and the legal order. Bearing in mind the unity of the Hungarian nation, Hungary shall bear responsibility for the fate of Hungarians living beyond its borders, facilitate the survival and development of their communities, support their efforts to preserve their Hungarian identity, to assert their individual and collective rights, and to ensure their welfare in their native lands and also promote their cooperation with one another and with Hungarians living in Hungary.' (Articles A–D of the Fundamental Law of Hungary) [47].

It is worth noting that the constitution did not introduce any new fundamental constitutional arrangements, focusing instead on certain corrective elements. Notably, the number of deputies in the National Assembly was reduced from 386 to 199. Hungary has a mixed parliamentary electoral system. With the adoption of the new constitution in 2011, the second round of voting was abolished. Under the current system, 106 deputies are elected in single-member constituencies, while 93 are elected from national party lists. Thus, each voter casts two votes: one for an individual candidate and one for a party list. The constitution also clarified the competences and organisational structure of the state administration, introducing a tighter centralisation of state power. The term of office for local authorities was extended from four to five years [47].

In contemporary Hungary, the political turning point was not initiated by constitutional regulations. In the summer of 2014, Prime Minister Viktor Orbán declared his intention to build an illiberal democracy in his country, drawing inspiration from countries such as Turkey, Russia, and Kazakhstan. As noted by Bogdan Góralczyk, a Polish expert on Hungary, upon returning to power in the spring of 2010, Orbán's camp took four key steps: (1) it named the new political order the 'System of National Cooperation' (*Nemzeti Együttműködési Rendszer* – NER), grounding it in a sense of solidarity and citizens' duties towards the national community rather than in affiliation to the state; (2) accordingly, 4 June – the date of the signing of the Trianon Treaty, a traumatic event for the Hungarian people as it divided their country following the First World War – was immediately declared a national holiday in 2010, and members of the extensive Hungarian diaspora in the neighbouring countries (estimated at between 2.2 and 2.5 million) were granted citizenship, followed a few years later by voting rights; (3) a new media order was introduced in the country with the aim of building government-controlled national media; (4) and finally, a new constitution was drafted [48]. The constitution and constitutional principles became subordinate to the imperative of keeping the ruling bloc in power. Analysts view the developments in Hungary and the rise of illiberal tendencies in a broader global and European context (Russia, Turkey, China, Kazakhstan) [19, 49]. Ivan Krastev and Stephen Holmes have argued that the observed decline in the appeal of the liberal democratic model stems partly from the uncritical adoption of the socio-political and economic solutions from Western Europe and the United States during the systemic transformation. The 2008 economic crisis and the subsequent crisis of European integration – which followed the migration crisis and the Covid-19 pandemic – led to a loss of faith in Euro-Atlantic solutions as inherently superior and as guarantees of a more prosperous life. At the same time, growing public disillusionment with the established political elites has eroded trust in representative democracy, as reflected in the emergence of new parties, often with anti-establishment profiles, and dwindling voter turnout in general elections. Public dissatisfaction with the ruling elites is increasing; they are frequently accused of inefficiency, hypocrisy, and greed. Allegations of corruption are mounting as well. This has created a social climate marked by uncertainty and anticipation of a radical political shift. Therefore, it appears that even stable constitutional arrangements do not guarantee the stability of a political system – as illustrated by the repeated failure to form a governing majority in Bulgaria since 2022, or the undemocratic tendencies seen in Poland and Hungary since 2015 [50–54].

Another key issue, alongside constitutional provisions, is constitutional practice. In this regard, the experience of the discussed region throughout the twentieth century offers little cause for optimism. In Poland, following the May Coup of 1926, an extraconstitutional centre of state power emerged in the person of Marshal Józef Piłsudski. Although he formally served only as Minister of Military Affairs, he was effectively in charge of the Polish state. In the Republic of Czechoslovakia, democratic identity remained more faithful to constitutional norms. However, the country saw the formation of an informal body known as the 'Pětka,' comprising the leaders of the five major political parties, who, together with the President of the Republic, made key decisions on state matters. In Romania and Bulgaria, real power rested with the court camarilla and military commanders, as evidenced by numerous coups and political upheavals, such as the 1934 coup in Bulgaria and the establishment of royal dictatorship in Romania in 1938. Meanwhile, Hungary installed a conservative regency regime, which only nominally restored the constitutional arrangements of the Austro-Hungarian period (1867–1918).

Even after the Second World War and the establishment of the Soviet sphere of influence in Central and Eastern Europe, constitutional practice diverged significantly from the letter of the law. Most notably, the Soviet model, implemented in various forms across Central and Eastern Europe, involved the creation of extraconstitutional centres of state power in the form of central and regional structures of the communist parties. The Politburo functioned as the equivalent of a government, while the Central Committee acted as a *de facto* representative body. These organs fundamentally distorted the model enshrined in the constitution, which formally established parliamentary supremacy over the other branches of state power. The most visible consequence was the lack of judicial independence and impartiality. With only minor adjustments over time, this model remained in place until its collapse in the late 1990s.

This is why shaping a democratic constitutional order in this region after 1989 posed such a significant challenge. It is worth noting that efforts were made to draw on political institutions from Western Europe, particularly consolidated democratic models such as France's Fifth Republic and Germany's chancellor system. However, the legacy of past undemocratic experiences often proved more resilient. The constitutional practice of the 'democrature' in Slovakia under Mečiar's rule, most notably the government's efforts to weaken the real position of the president, offers a clear example. Similar undemocratic tendencies marked the early years of Romania's constitution under post-communist rule until the autumn of 1996. Constitutional practice in Bulgaria must also be assessed negatively, especially during the rule of Boyko Borisov, which became a symbol of the fusion of politics, business, and organised crime. In the Polish context after 2015, it is necessary to highlight the problematic recurrent practice of forming an extraconstitutional centre of power in the person of the leader of the victorious party (Law and Justice), who operated above the constitutionally defined offices of Prime Minister and President. This directly echoed the political arrangements from the period following the 1926 coup and from the People's Republic. Post-2010 Hungary provides the most extensive example of constitutional practice diverging from the letter of the law. The curtailment of judicial power, media freedom, and the scope of local governance created a scenario in which real power was concentrated in a strong, largely unchecked executive centred on the Prime Minister and the state administration [55–57].

6. Conclusions

This analysis has examined the most recent constitutional trends in the countries of Central and Eastern Europe. Over the course of the twentieth century, the region experienced multiple systemic transformations: shifts towards parliamentary democracy, periods of military authoritarianism, transitions into people's

Poland	Hungary	Czechoslovakia	Bulgaria	Romania
Democracy of the Parliament (1921)	Parliamentary monarchy with regent (1920)	Parliamentary and cabinet democracy (1920)	Constitutional/ parliamentary monarchy (1879)	Parliamentary monarchy (1923)
Presidential authoritarianism (1935)	Parliamentary Model (1946)	Hybrid regime (1948)	State of People's Democracy (1947)	Royal dictatorship (1938)
Państwo People's Democracy (1952)	State of People's Democracy (1949)	The Socialist State (1960)	The Socialist State (1971)	State of People's Democracy (1948)
The Socialist State (1976)	The Socialist State (1972)	Parliamentary and cabinet democracy (Czech Republic, 1992)	Parliamentary and Cabinet Democracy (1991)	The Socialist State (1965)
Hybrid model (parliamentary-presidential) 1989	Model of Parliamentary Democracy (1989)	Parliamentary and cabinet democracy (Slovak Republic, 1992)		Parliamentary and presidential democracy (1991)
The parliamentary-cabinet model with a strengthened role of the government (1997)	Parliamentary and cabinet model with a strengthened position of the Government (2011)			

Source: Own study.

Table 1.
Political evolution of Central and Eastern European countries in the twentieth century.

democracies and socialism during the dominance of the USSR, and, finally, democratic transformations at the turn of the 1980s and 1990s (**Table 1**). Alongside the shared trajectories of socio-political and, to a similar extent, economic development, there were significant divergences, reflected in the durability of democratic political institutions in pre-war Czechoslovakia and the varied models of socialist states, including more liberal iterations of communist rule in Poland after 1956, Hungary after 1962, Yugoslavia after 1948, and Czechoslovakia between 1963 and 1968. Post-communist transitions were also far from linear, with diverse scenarios in the evolution of the political, social, and economic situation. Nevertheless, a number of common elements can be seen in the analysed constitutional processes, as discussed above [56]. Following the adoption of new constitutional acts (primarily in the first half of the 1990s, with the exception of Poland and Hungary), several countries introduced direct presidential elections, including Poland in 1990, Slovakia in 1998, and the Czech Republic in 2012. At the same time, they established broad catalogues of human and civil rights, based on universal instruments adopted by the United Nations and the Council of Europe (and later, the EU). The Czech Republic incorporated the Charter of Fundamental Rights and Freedoms, adopted by the Czechoslovak parliament in January 1991. New constitutional provisions referred to international alliances and European institutions, particularly in the context of transferring certain state competences. As part of preparations for EU accession, individual countries refined their regulations related to judicial independence and the autonomy of the judiciary. In parallel, drawing on domestic constitutional and socio-political traditions, they restored historical institutions (such as bicameral parliaments – the Senate in Poland, the Czech Republic, and Romania), state names (Republic of Poland, Hungary, Romania), and national emblems and symbols. This trend is especially pronounced in the most recent constitution adopted in the region: Hungary's Fundamental Law of 2011 [58].

Author details

Jacek Wojnicki
Department of Political Systems, Faculties of Political Sciences and International Studies, Warsaw University, Warsaw, Poland

*Address all correspondence to: jacekwojnicki@uw.edu.pl

References

[1] Agh Attila. The Politics of Central Europe. London: Sage Publications; 1998

[2] Działocha K, Mojak R, Wójtowicz K. Ten Years of the Democratic Constitutionalism in Central and Eastern Europe. Lublin: Morpol; 2001

[3] Mink G, Szurek J-M. Cet Étrange Post-communisme. Rupture Et Transition En Europe Central Et Orientale. Paris: CNRS Edition; 1992

[4] Antoszewski A, Herbut R. Demokracje Europy Środkowo-wschodniej W Perspektywie Porównawczej: Wrocław; Uniwersytet Wrocławski; 1997

[5] Kofman J, Roszkowski W. Transformacja I Postkomunizm. Warszawa: Instytut Studiów Politycznych PAN; 1999

[6] Wojtaszczyk A, Godlewski T, Koseski A. Transformacja Systemowa W Krajach Europy Środkowej, Wschodniej I Południowej 1989-2002. Wybrane Problemy. Bydgoszcz-Pułtusk; 2003

[7] Wojnicki J. Trudna Droga Do Demokracji. Europa Środkowo-wschodnia Po 1989. Warszawa: Instytut Nauk Politycznych UW; 2002

[8] Szymczak T. Ustrój Europejskich Państw Socjalistycznych. Warszawa: Państwowe Wydawnictwo Naukowe; 1988

[9] Bankowicz M. Transformacje Konstytucyjnych Systemów Władzy Państwowej W Europie Środkowej. Kraków: Wydawnictwo Uniwersytetu Jagiellońskiego; 2010

[10] Zawadzka B. Zmiany Systemu Politycznego W Ustawodawstwie Państw Europy Środkowej I Wschodniej. Warszawa: Wydawnictwo Naukowe Scholar; 1992

[11] Vrabie G. Le Régime Politique Et Constitutionnel de la Roumanie Post-décembriste. Bucureşti: Institutul European; 2021

[12] Mołdawa T. Państwo I Ustrój. Zagadnienia Systemów Rządów I Instytucji Politycznych. Warszawa: Elipsa; 2018

[13] Wyrzykowski M. Recepcja w prawie publicznym – Tendencje rozwojowe konstytucjonalizmu w Europie Środkowej i Wschodniej. Państwo I Prawo. 1992;11

[14] Bujwid-Kurek E. Serbia W Nowej Przestrzeni Ustrojowej. Kraków: Księgarnia Akademicka; 2012

[15] Holmes Stephen T. O metodzie zmian konstytucyjnych w państwach Europy Wschodniej. Państwo I Prawo. 1993;8

[16] Kruk M. Konstytucja: Prawo I Praktyka. Warszawa: Wydawnictwo Sejmowe; 2018

[17] Fejto F. La Fin Des Démocraties Populaires. Paris: Le Seuil; 1992

[18] Guida F. L'altra Metà dell'Europa. Dalla Grande Guerra Ai Giorni Nostri. Roma-Bari: Editori Laterza; 2020

[19] Kiełmiński Z. Współczesne Systemy Polityczne. Wybrane Zagadnienia. Warszawa: Elipsa; 2022

[20] Żmigrodzki M. Przeobrażenia Polityczno-ustrojowe I Sąd Konstytucyjny W Bułgarii. Lublin: Wydawnictwo Uniwersytetu Marii Curie-Skłodowskiej; 1997

[21] Sokolewicz W. Wokół Konstytucji. Pisma Wybrane. Warszawa: Wolters Kluwer business; 2011

[22] Gebethner S. Państwo-Demokracja -Konstytucja. Warszawa: Wydawnictwo Sejmowe; 2022

[23] Chruściak R. Bułgaria. Konstytucja Bułgarii uchwalona 12 lipca 1991 r. seria: Przemiany konstytucyjne w Europie Wschodniej. Vol. **1**. Warszawa: Elipsa; 1993

[24] Karp J. Konstytucja Republiki Bułgarii. Warszawa: Wydawnictwo Sejmowe; 2012

[25] Brodziński W. Konstytucja Rumunii Z 21 Listopada 1991 R. Warszawa: Wydawnictwo Sejmowe; 1996

[26] Bankowicz M. Systemy Władzy Państwowej Czechosłowacji I Czech. Kraków: PIT; 1998

[27] Kruk M. Konstytucja Republiki Czeskiej. Warszawa: Wydawnictwo Sejmowe; 1994

[28] Skotnicki K. System Konstytucyjny Czech. Warszawa: Wydawnictwo Sejmowe; 2000

[29] Donath H. Konstytucja Republiki Węgierskiej. Warszawa: Wydawnictwo Sejmowe; 1996

[30] Ludwikowski Rett R. Prawo Konstytucyjne Porównawcze. Toruń: TNOiK; 2000

[31] Brodziński W. System Konstytucyjny Węgier. Warszawa: Wydawnictwo Sejmowe; 2003

[32] Simko I. A Vyhnali Mečiara. Dramatický Príbeh Porážky Mečiarizmu. Žilina: Artis Omnis; 2018

[33] Filip J. Ústavní Právo. Brno: Masarykova univerziteta; 2015

[34] Giba Marián a Kolektív. Ústavné Právo. Bratislava: Wolters Kluwer; 2019

[35] Starzewski M. Środki Zabezpieczenia Prawnego Konstytucyjności Ustaw. Warszawa: Wydawnictwo Sejmowe; 2009

[36] Garlicki L. Sądownictwo Konstytucyjne W Europie Zachodniej. Warszawa: Państwowe Wydawnictwo Naukowe; 1987

[37] Ludwikowska Anna M. Sądownictwo Konstytucyjne W Europie Środkowo-wschodniej W Okresie Przekształceń Demokratycznych. Studium Porównawcze. Toruń: TNOiK; 1997

[38] Hartwig M. The Institutionalization of the Rule of Law: The Establishment of Constitutional Courts in the Eastern European Countries. American University International Law Review. 1992;7(3):449–470

[39] Brodziński W. System Konstytucyjny Rumunii. Warszawa: Wydawnictwo Sejmowe; 2006

[40] Grzybowski M, Karp J. System Konstytucyjny Bułgarii. Warszawa: Wydawnictwo Sejmowe; 2002

[41] Kubuj K, Wawrzyniak J. Europeizacja Konstytucji Państw Unii Europejskiej. Warszawa: Wydawnictwo Naukowe Scholar; 2011

[42] Cibulka L. Ústavne Pravo. Ústávný System Slovenskey Republiky. Bratislava: Wolters Kluwer; 2007

[43] Pytlik B. Parlament I Rząd W Republice Słowackiej. Warszawa: Oficyna Szkoły Głównej Handlowej; 2013

[44] Pytlik B. Instytucja Prezydenta W Państwach Grupy Wyszehradzkiej. Warszawa: Elipsa; 2024

[45] Hejj D. Konstytucja Węgier jako manifest polityczny parlamentarnej większości. Przegląd Prawa Konstytucyjnego. 2018;(1):67–85

[46] Kopyś T. Ewolucja koncepcji narodu w węgierskiej polityce po 1989. Środkowoeuropejskie Studia Polityczne. 2025;(1):215–244

[47] Sadecki A. Ustawa Zasadnicza Węgier. Warszawa: Wydawnictwo Sejmowe; 2015

[48] Góralczyk B. Węgry: Zwrot Do Systemu Nieliberalnego. Rocznik Strategiczny; 2017/2018: 327–341 p.

[49] Wiatr Jerzy J. New Authoritarianism. Challenges to Democracy in the 21st Century. Opladen, Berlin, Toronto: Barbara Budrich Publishers; 2019

[50] Kamiński Antoni Z, Kamiński B. Świat Na Krawędzi. Czy Ustrój Liberalno-konstytucyjny Sprosta Wyzwaniom Współczesności. Kraków-Warszawa: Księgarnia Akademicka, Instytut Studiów Politycznych PAN; 2023

[51] Kubas S. Procesy Demokratyzacji I Jego Determinanty. Analiza Na Przykładzie Republiki Czeskiej I Węgier (1990-2016). Katowice; Wydawnictwo Uniwersytetu Śląskiego; 2018

[52] Zakaria F. Przyszłość Wolności. Nieliberalna Demokracja W Stanach Zjednoczonych I Na Świecie. Łódź; Kultura Liberalna; 2018

[53] Krastew Iwan. Demokracja: Przepraszamy Za Usterki. Warszawa: Krytyka Polityczna; 2015

[54] Kurlantzick J. Demokracja Liberalna W Odwrocie. Warszawa: Nowa Konfederacja; 2022

[55] Krastew I, Holmes S. Światło, Które Zgasło. Jak Zachód Zawiódł Swoich Wyznawców. Warszawa: Krytyka Polityczna; 2019

[56] Wiatr Jerzy J. Political Leadership between Democracy and Authoritarianism. Opladen, Berlin, Toronto: Barbara Budrich Publishers; 2022

[57] Lesko M. Mečiar a Mečiarizmus. Bratislava: VMV; 1997

[58] Staśkiewicz W. Konstytucje Państw Unii Europejskiej. Warszawa: Wydawnictwo Sejmowe; 2011

Section 3

Law Enforcement

Chapter 6

The Crisis of Confidence: Understanding the Effects of Police Corruption, Abuse and Brutality on Public Perceptions of Law Enforcement in Africa

Paul Oluwatosin Bello and Adewale A. Olutola

Abstract

This chapter contributes to the literature on police corruption, abuse, and brutality within Africa's security landscape by exploring their complexities across various African countries. Incidents of police corruption, abuse, and brutality are pervasive issues affecting many societies across African countries. While police authorities have introduced reforms and initiatives aimed at recalibrating and repositioning police institutions, the problems have persisted unabated. Instead of diminishing, the problem is escalating, resulting in extrajudicial killings, harassment, and the brutality of citizens. Drawing on a corpus of scholarly articles and publications, this chapter examines the complexities of police corruption, abuse, and brutality in many African societies. It identifies and discusses the key factors contributing to these issues and their effects on public confidence in law enforcement and proposes measures that can be adopted to address the problem.

Keywords: police corruption, abuse and brutality, confidence, Africa, Public

1. Introduction

Literature has widely reported on the importance of public perception of the police in effective policing in modern societies [1–3]. This understanding stems from the realisation that the police cannot operate in isolation from the public. The police are the most visible representatives of the state and the closest link between the government and the public. Charged with the responsibility of enforcing laws and maintaining order in society, the police wield enormous legal powers to compel obedience. However, despite the powers vested in them to prevent, combat, and investigate crimes as enacted in states' domestic legal and regulatory frameworks, these tasks cannot be achieved without public cooperation and support.

The public plays an important role in influencing behaviour and maintaining order through informal social control mechanisms, including social norms, community expectations, and public opinion. This conception has spurred increased interest among policymakers, academics, students, and other relevant stakeholders in promoting public support for the police. This perspective has also led to a plethora of research on public perception, cooperation, and support for the police in different parts of the world [1, 2, 4–6]. While the findings of most of these studies have implications for policing, particularly in fostering public support for the police, there is a need to highlight some grey areas that considerably impede public support for the police, especially in Africa, which require attention. These areas (among others) revolve around major unethical practices and misconduct by the police, such as police corruption, abuse, and brutality.

Public trust and confidence in the police are currently low and declining in most African countries due to certain unethical practices by the police, as seen in countries like South Africa, where only about 27% of citizens express some trust in the police [7-9]. The findings from a recent survey of 39 African countries (conducted between 2021 and 2023) further established that Africans generally have a low regard for the quality of policing on the continent [10, 11]. These indicators suggest that people are not satisfied with the services rendered by the police, based on their encounters, experiences, and interactions with the police, which may significantly impact their confidence in the police.

Police corruption, abuse, and brutality are endemic problems across many African societies [10–13], undermining police professionalism, the rule of law, threatening internal safety and security, and eroding public confidence in law enforcement. These acts of misconduct not only besmirch the reputation of the principal law enforcement institution but also have significant negative implications for public perception of the police. While some authors have censured and attributed these unethical practices and misconduct to a 'few bad apples', that is, a small number of individuals (officers) within the institution [14–17], others have identified them as widespread problems that have severely damaged most police institutions across the African continent [2, 3, 18–23].

It is challenging to measure or determine the extent of police corruption, abuse, and brutality in Africa owing to certain factors. These factors include, but are not limited to, regional dynamics, underreporting – especially among marginalised groups/communities due to intimidation and fear of reprisals – varying policing environments, and complex police practices and experiences [24, 25]. However, there are anecdotes on the prevalence of police corruption and violence in different regions of Africa [26–28]. Reliable evidence in recent times points to the fact that many African societies have experienced a rise in police misconduct and violence, including corruption, extrajudicial killings, use of excessive force, torture, and sexual violence [1, 26, 29–32]. For example, the New York Times [33] documented frequent media reports of unprofessional conduct, corruption, selective law enforcement practices, unlawful arrests, use of excessive force, and other human rights abuses by the police in Africa.

Why have these snags persisted and worsened in many African countries despite the propagation of community policing and other innovative policing models across the globe? What are the underlying factors that contribute to these problems, and how can they be addressed? Using secondary academic sources from a corpus of literature, this chapter examines the enigma of police corruption, abuse, and brutality in Africa. From a positional standpoint, the chapter attempts to conceptualise police corruption, abuse, and brutality from an African perspective, discuss key contributing factors to these enigmas, and propose measures that can be adopted to combat the problem.

2. Conceptualising police corruption, abuse, and brutality in Africa

Conceptualising these concepts in Africa requires a profound understanding of their multifaceted nature, historical and systemic origins, organisational dynamics, socio-political contexts, and diverse manifestations across the continent. Although common threads exist, their forms may vary from region to region and from one African country to another.

2.1 Police corruption

Police corruption, as defined by Roebuck and Barker, can broadly be described as 'a deviant, dishonest, improper, unethical or criminal behaviour by a police officer' [34]. It is also broadly defined as 'the abuse of police power for personal gain' [35]. Such abuse manifests in different forms, often when police exploit their discretionary powers for personal gain. Police are consistently ranked among the most corrupt public institutions in Africa [11, 34]. The recent Afro-Barometer survey report on police corruption in Africa indicates that 'almost half (46%) of citizens of 39 African countries say "most" or "all" police officials are corrupt, the worst rating among 11 public institutions' [11, 36]. In many African societies, being stopped by the police without justification or a traffic regulation violation is often a prelude to bribery solicitation, whether overt or covert [37–39].

Securing police support or assistance in Africa often comes with a price. Such support often involves citizens parting with cash through unrealistic handshakes, under-the-table tips, and cash transfers [40]. In most cases, people often prefer to settle or comply with the police's demands to avoid being framed for a crime or offense and to prevent harassment or abuse from the officers on duty. For example, 36% of the 2021/2023 Afro-barometer survey participants say they had to pay a bribe to the police to get the help they needed [11, 36]. In other results from the same survey, from the 13% of participants who say they asked for police assistance during the previous year, 36% of them say they were asked to pay a bribe, give a gift, or do a favour to get the assistance they needed from the police [11, 36]. These types of interactions when seeking assistance were most common in Liberia (78%), Nigeria (75%), Sierra Leone (72%), and Uganda (71%), and least common in Seychelles (4%), Mauritius (3%), and Cape Verde (2%) [11]. Among those who encountered the police in other situations, 37% report having to pay a bribe to avoid problems, ranging from 1% in Cape Verde to 70% in Liberia [11]. Citizens who argue or resist the 'men in blue or black' during such encounters often risk being harassed, abused, intimidated, and, in extreme cases, killed. Although the forms of police corruption in Africa are very broad, the dominant ones include:

[i] **Small-scale or petty corruption:** this is the commonest form of police corruption in Africa. It involves law enforcement officials soliciting minor bribes, kickbacks, or favours in return for disregarding minor

infractions, evading prosecution, or expediting services [41–44]. For example, it is commonplace in many African societies for the police to solicit 'tolls' from commuters at checkpoints. The codenames, terms, or slang used by the police in making such demands vary from one African country to another. For instance, in Nigeria, it is '*egunje*' or '*roja me*', and in South Africa, it is '*money for coke*'. Regardless of the phrases used, such practices are pervasive in many African cosmopolitan cities, and governments seem to be helpless in addressing the menace [45, 46]. Petty corruption by police officers also involves receiving bribes to turn a blind eye to or dismiss traffic violations, or extorting cash from vendors [37, 47]. This is presumably the most common type of police corruption in Africa [48].

[ii] **Grand corruption**: This typically involves higher-ranking police officers or those working in tandem with organised crime groups and involves larger quantities of money or substantial benefits [17, 43, 44]. This type of police corruption manifests when police officers attempt to cover up crimes or criminal activities such as human or drug trafficking, fraud, or falsifying or fabricating evidence in major cases, to mention a few [13, 17].

[iii] **Extortion and shakedowns**: Police officers in many African countries solicit bribes or demand payments from individuals, often under the threat of arrest, physical harm, or falsified charges [2, 26, 49, 50]. Most targets of the police for this type of corruption are vulnerable populations, such as undocumented migrants, sex workers, and informal traders [51–53].

[iv] **'Fixing' cases**: Police officers sometimes engage in unlawful practices, undermining criminal prosecutions by accepting bribes or other benefits in exchange for actions such as withholding evidence, failing to appear in court, or altering testimony [54]. This conduct sabotages the integrity of the justice system by deliberately obstructing the lawful process of prosecution and trial [2, 22].

[v] **Internal payoffs**: This type of police corruption thrives within police agencies and manifests in the form of racketeering, in which promotions, positions, and postings within police institutions are bought and sold [43, 55, 56]. This organisational corruption is deeply rooted in most police institutions across the continent and has significant implications for police effectiveness. It is the practice of monetising positions or opportunities within an institution based on a vantage point for personal gain [57].

[vi] **Nepotism and clientelism**: These concepts are two sides of the same coin. Nepotism in law enforcement institutions occurs when recruitment, placement, appointment, promotion, or benefits are influenced by connections or family relationships rather than merit, qualifications, performance, or experience [1, 58]. When unqualified officials are

promoted based on connections rather than merit, it leads to incompetent policing, low morale among dedicated and honest officers, and a decline in public trust. Relatedly, clientelism, as a form of police corruption, refers to a situation or system in which police officers or officials develop and sustain networks of reciprocal favours, in the form of promotions or other benefits, as rewards for political support, cooperation, loyalty, or personal gain [44, 59].

2.2 Police abuse and brutality

Besides corruption, police abuse and brutality are pervasive in most African societies. Police abuse and brutality refer to the misuse or overuse of legitimate police powers, which manifests through unwarranted or excessive use of physical force, violence, or torture by law enforcement officers against civilians in ways that contravene the rules of engagement, procedural justice, and violate human rights. While overlapping with corruption, these two distinct yet complementary concepts encompass a broader range of misconduct, including the abuse of power, authority, or discretion; intimidation and harassment; violation of due process; non-responsiveness; negligence; and the use of excessive force [1]. This misconduct also includes the use of physical assault and beatings, ill-treatment and torture, and extrajudicial killings [21]. Police officials or officers in many African countries wield immense power and are known to abuse their authority when performing their constitutional duties [1, 26].

The history of police abuse and brutality in most parts of Africa predates the independence era, where the police were known for subjugation and suppression, ready to crush any opposition to colonial rule [60]. Law enforcement practices during this period were often predatory and ruthless, primarily driven by the asymmetric power relations between the principal law enforcement institution and its citizens [61]. However, the problem has persisted in most post-independence African societies, despite global calls for police reforms, accountability, and transformation. Although there might be variations in the extent and experiences across various African cultures and regions, police abuse and brutality remain endemic on the continent [60].

In response to global calls for police reforms, several African states have restructured their policing systems, including changing the nomenclature of their police institutions from 'police force' to 'police service' [62], and have even introduced community policing and other models to signal transformation in their respective countries' police institutional architecture [60, 63]. Yet, incidents of police abuse and brutality have persisted and remained unabated in most African societies today, besmirching police institutional reputation and image, and eroding public confidence in law enforcement [60]. Scholars have associated such failure with the previously highlighted historical colonial legacy of authoritarian policing that was rooted in control, suppression, and use of excessive force [1, 60]. It is therefore unsurprising that, while many African countries have long gained independence and claimed to adhere to democratic principles which promote the rule of law and respect for fundamental human rights, policing in most parts of the continent today still reflects some of the structural practices akin to colonial policing.

In most postcolonial African societies, law enforcement has often been hijacked by state machinery, the ruling political class, politicians, and other 'powerful' elites [64, 65]. The police are tools of intimidation, suppression, and harassment used by government officials to clamp down on their political opponents, activists, and citizens who criticise, oppose, or challenge their policies [66, 67]. During elections, police officers assigned to polling units often collude with agents of the ruling political party to subvert justice and compromise the electoral process [67]. They are complicit in electoral fraud, voter intimidation, and harassment of opposition agents and anyone who challenges their illegalities [68].

Public peaceful protests against unpopular government policies, poor service delivery, discrimination, human rights violations, ethnic-related issues, and other social enigmas are often met with resistance by state police, who arrest, intimidate, suppress, brutalise and adopt other unprofessional approaches in dispersing protestors, including young people [3, 69]. In most of these episodes, weapons such as batons, tasers, and firearms are used, even in non-threatening situations, inflicting injuries on people. It is commonplace in many African societies to see overzealous and trigger-excited police officers fire live ammunition and teargas at protestors and unleash terror on unarmed civilians who agitate for better governance. For example, the #EndSARS protests in Nigeria were met with resistance by the police, leading to the deaths of several citizens at the Lekki toll gate in Lagos [70, 71]. In South Africa, police brutality led to the deaths of 34 mine workers in Marikana in August 2012, commonly referred to as 'the Marikana Massacre' [72]. Additionally, the recent untimely deaths of Andries Tatane, Nathaniel Julius, and Mthokozisi Ntumba exemplify the ongoing issue of police brutality in the country [21]. Apart from these examples, there are several other accounts of police abuse and brutality in other parts of Africa [73–80].

Excessive force by the police has resulted in the deaths of many citizens across African societies [73–80]. Those arrested and taken into custody by the police are ill-treated, tortured, and brutalised [73–80]. More worrisome is that victims or relatives of victims of police violence hardly receive justice [81]. Cases of police brutality and fatalities are sometimes trivialised and not thoroughly investigated or prosecuted. Police officers who are culpable in such unprofessional acts are also not held accountable for their actions [26, 66], allowing such a cycle of violence to fester.

Contemporarily, there are catalogues of incidents of police abuse and brutality across many African societies [73–80, 82]. In relative terms, police officials in many African countries often perceive citizens as technically 'inferior' subjects who must obey or carry out their orders, regardless of the lawfulness or unlawfulness of such orders. Victims of police abuse and brutality are usually the poor, vulnerable, and ordinary citizens whom the police are supposed to protect. If you do not belong to the aristocratic class, or you are unconnected to the government, political class, or an influential person in society who is close to the seat of power in Africa, you are likely to be a victim of police abuse and brutality. You are also likely to be a victim of police abuse and brutality in African societies or have a vicarious experience of police violence if you fail to obey or comply with police orders or cooperate with the police. All these have significant implications for undermining human rights, justice, legitimacy, and public trust in law enforcement institutions.

3. Methodology

The chapter adopts a reflective positional perspective in explaining the effects of police corruption, abuse, and brutality on public perception of law enforcement in Africa. This approach is rooted in the interpretivist epistemological standpoint and stems from the broader qualitative method. Qualitative scholars are expected to be critically reflective in their approach to knowledge production and transmission [83]. Since researchers form an integral part of qualitative academic processes, it is essential to understand their positions within a particular academic discourse. They are expected to explain their positionality to readers of their work from an actively reflective standpoint while ensuring transparency in analysing sensitive phenomena, such as institutional misconduct [84].

The research design (interpretivist) synthesises secondary qualitative data through systematic thematic analysis, focusing on exploratory and explanatory insights into perceptual dynamics. Data sources for this chapter include peer-reviewed articles, Afrobarometer surveys, Human Rights Watch reports, and various African case studies, accessed via databases such as Google Scholar and JSTOR. These data were analysed, interpreted, and discussed from a reflective positional standpoint to provide an understanding of the complexity of police corruption, abuse, and brutality in Africa, and how they shape public trust in law enforcement institutions.

4. Key factors contributing to police corruption, abuse, and brutality in Africa

The key factors contributing to police corruption, abuse, and brutality in Africa can be classified into three broad categories: Individual, institutional, and societal. Complex socioeconomic and institutional milieus within many African societies facilitate these factors, which collectively erode police integrity and accountability.

From an individual perspective, low moral values, greed, obsession with power and control, and sometimes sadistic tendencies among police officers are frequently cited as some of the drivers of corruption, citizen abuse, and brutality in Africa [40, 63, 64]. Police officers often abuse their positions for personal gain through bribery and other illegitimate activities [40, 63, 64]. Personal ambitions and ulterior motives sometimes fuel the unethical practices of police officers. Despite the training, orientation, and other support provided by the institution's authorities upon recruitment, their ulterior motives or self-interest often conflict with institutional ethics [43]. Such ulterior motives and selfish ambitions, coupled with poor accountability or oversight mechanisms and inadequate training, exacerbate corruption tendencies among police officers, sometimes putting them under pressure to resist bribes and use clandestine means to enforce compliance or assert their authority [43, 44, 85, 86].

At the organisational level, police institutions in many African countries often lack robust oversight and accountability systems for addressing errant or corrupt officers [43, 87]. Such gaps enable corruption and other unethical practices to thrive. They also promote a culture of impunity, where corrupt and other unethical acts perpetrated by police officers go unpunished. Additionally, systemic structural problems, such as dysfunctional anti-corruption units, inadequate internal reporting mechanisms, low remuneration, and poor working conditions, among others, within institutions, create opportunities for systemic corruption, abuse of power, and police violence [88, 89]. The perceived normalisation of corrupt acts and other forms of misconduct among personnel can embed unethical practices in the institutional culture [85]. Additionally, weak institutional support and an inadequate welfare system also contribute to the prevalence of corruption and other unethical practices by police officers [90, 91]. These structural gaps negatively impact police officers' psyche, morale, and attitude to work, making them react irrationally in public and act unethically when interacting with citizens [85].

Police officers in many African countries receive poor remuneration compared to their counterparts in other parts of the world and in the public sector [92]. Some reside in dilapidated buildings, and they can barely survive on their meagre salaries. Police barracks in some African countries are among the most deplorable living conditions for civil servants. To survive, some low-ranked or junior officers engage in unethical practices, such as setting up illegal roadblocks or checkpoints where they extort commercial drivers and other commuters, while others engage in unlawful activities [85, 93]. These officers are sometimes aggressive towards non-complying commuters or citizens and sometimes harass or react violently in the process, which often results in altercations and brutality. Excessive use of force by police might have contributed to several fatalities across African societies. Institutional frustrations sometimes drive such misconduct.

Police corruption, abuse, and brutality in Africa also stem from societal and economic factors [20, 48]. While we have highlighted the effect of individual and institutional factors on this problem, we cannot overlook the role played by societal and economic factors. There is an entrenched societal tolerance for corruption in many African societies, rooted in the perception that services cannot be rendered or offered without a bribe or tip [90]. This entrenched corrupt notion has significantly influenced police officers. Beyond rhetoric, corruption has been institutionalised in many African societies [23, 94]. Citizens sometimes hold the view that they need to bribe or influence public officials to achieve their desired goals, thereby compromising established institutions and legal authorities [87]. In relative terms, citizens of many African countries are active participants in corruption processes [95]. Police interactions with a 'corrupting public' often create an enabling environment for corruption.

Economic hardships further exacerbate this situation, making it challenging for police officers to rely solely on one stream of income. The lure of extra income might, therefore, tempt officers to engage in corrupt exchanges [43]. However, research suggests that salary levels alone do not provide a uniform explanation for police corruption in all African societies, as police sometimes earn more than other public servants [37, 43]. Public distrust in police professionalism and widespread perceptions of corruption negatively affect public cooperation and confidence in law enforcement [96].

The enigma of police abuse and brutality in Africa further stems from the effects of a 'corrupt public' and the institutionalisation of corruption. The Afro-Barometer survey report indicates that 'only about one-third (32%) of Africans say their police "often" or "always" operate in a professional manner and respect the rights of all citizens. This figure ranges from a low of 13% in Nigeria to a high of 58% in Burkina Faso' [11]. Police abuse and brutality are the offshoots of police corruption. Triggers of police abuse and brutality include refusing to give in or consent to police officers' demands for a bribe, non-cooperation from a 'corrupt public', disapproval of certain police actions, dissatisfaction with the procedures adopted by the police in managing conflicts or handling public unrest, and demanding explanations for specific police actions. In many African societies, police officers are often perceived as authoritative and domineering, unwilling to be accountable or take responsibility for their actions [43, 60, 97]. Such traits stem from their historical or colonial legacy of suppression rather than protection. In many African countries, the police have used tear gas on protesters during peaceful protests, despite not violating any rules of engagement. They are often captured on camera assaulting or brutalising citizens for violating traffic rules or disobeying their orders [98, 99]. Some trigger-happy police officers have shot at unarmed civilians, and at times, passer-by have been hit by stray bullets, resulting in fatalities [45].

The above actions are by-products of poor or insufficient training and skills. Research reveals that many African countries provide inadequate or substandard training to their police officers [20, 100]. The effect of substandard training is reflected in their poor approaches to issues in public spaces. Many police officers lack the skills, abilities, and depth of professionalism necessary to manage and resolve conflicts in a peaceful and mutually agreeable manner for all parties involved [101]. Oftentimes, the outcome of police interventions worsens the situation and turns minor issues into more complicated ones, resulting in the use of excessive force. The de-escalation of public protests by the police in Africa has often snowballed into full-scale violence due to poor training [1, 102].

Often, police misconduct in Africa goes unpunished, even when considerable efforts are made by the public, the media, and civil organisations to draw the attention of police authorities to it [66]. Police authorities in many African countries have an impressive profile of engaging in institutional damage control when they should take responsibility for the actions of their erring officials [74, 103]. Weak accountability systems and oversight foster a culture of impunity [66, 85, 94]. Scholars have criticised the effectiveness of oversight bodies established in many African countries to handle police misconduct [66, 85, 94]. For example, authors have averred that the absence of an accountability system within the South African Police Service (SAPS) serves as a key driver of widespread police brutality in the country [21, 104].

The effect of environmental and work-related stressors on police abuse and brutality in many African countries cannot be overemphasized [105–107]. Police officers in most African societies often work in violent, hostile, and crime-ridden environments with inadequate resources, poor remuneration, and psychological stress [107, 108]. Organisational coping mechanisms are also relatively poor [107]. Poor remuneration and poor working conditions not only facilitate corruption but also contribute to it. They also create an atmosphere for police officers to engage in brutality, either as an enforcement tactic or as part of criminal collusion.

Although unpronounced in the public domain, many police officers in Africa experience and suffer from severe psychological/mental health issues, resulting in post-traumatic stress disorder (PTSD) and other stressors owing to their job-occupation demands and high exposure to violence [107]. Such experiences often trigger aggression in them and contribute to their abusive behaviour. All these actions erode public confidence and satisfaction with the police [102, 109]. They also undermine law enforcement effectiveness, allowing crime to flourish and eroding the rule of law in many African contexts. Corruption at all levels, including among senior officials, disrupts police legitimacy and public safety, posing substantial threats to governance and democratic consolidation [94].

5. The effects of police corruption, abuse, and brutality on public trust in the police in Africa

Police corruption, abuse, and brutality exert deep, multi-layered effects on public trust in law enforcement across African countries, undermining its legitimacy, weakening states' capacity to control crime, and eroding public compliance with the law and the cooperation necessary for effective policing [2, 3, 9]. Where police are perceived to be corrupt, violent, or unprofessional, citizens often withdraw cooperation, report crime less, and increasingly view the police as a threat rather than a protector [3, 109, 110]. Based on the previously discussed Afrobarometer surveys conducted across 39 African countries, misconduct by law enforcement officials is associated with low levels of trust in the police [11, 36].

Public trust in the police is built, among other things, on the perceived procedural fairness and legitimacy of police officers. As a legal authority, the police are expected to conduct themselves responsibly and treat citizens with respect and dignity. Such expectations engender police legitimacy and promote cooperation for social control. However, when the public perceives the police as unfair and rude, their trust in them declines.

Corruption is arguably one of the strongest predictors of low public trust in the police across African societies [111]. Afrobarometer data shows that nearly half (46%) of Africans believe that 'most' or 'all' police officers are corrupt, the worst rating among all public institutions surveyed [11, 36]. When the public holds the view that the police are corrupt, and by extension serve their own interests and those of the elite or the powerful in society, rather than those of the public, it has a long-term impact on their trust in law enforcement [9, 59]. Such perceptions often make people reluctant to report crimes, support or assist investigations, or cooperate with the police due to fear of being ignored, victimised, or forced to pay bribes [112]. It also fosters the perception among people that the law is biased and favours only the wealthy [43]. These perceptions fuel distrust in the police and account for why people sometimes take the law into their own hands, carrying out policing functions illegitimately [9].

6. Impact of abuse and brutality

Police abuse and brutality, in addition to corruption, directly blight the image of the police before the public. From the findings of Afrobarometer, in many African countries, people say that police use too much force when dealing with suspects (42%) and during protests (38%) [11]. They also say that police officers often get away with their actions [11]. Prominent incidents of police brutality in African communities, such as the shooting of passersby through stray bullets, the murder of suspects in custody, or public protesters, are widely reported and have become portrayals of state carnage, deepening public distrust, fear, and resentment [1, 21, 113].

Brutality portends that the police are not bound by the law they are supposed to enforce. When people see or experience police violence, they are less likely to view the police as legitimate authority figures and more likely to see them as part of the problem. Such a condition becomes precarious in milieus where the image of the police institution is already blighted due to their misconduct. It also affirms the notion that the police are active participants or culpable in the commission of crime and dishonest in their engagements with the public.

7. Link to low professionalism and legitimacy

Police corruption, abuse, and brutality are closely tied to low public trust across the continent. Afrobarometer finds that only about one in three Africans (32%) say their police usually operate in a professional manner and respect citizens' rights [11]. In many African countries, trust in the police is low [11].

Citizens feel no moral obligation to obey or assist the police because they believe the police are acting unfairly and against the public interest. This weakens the social contract between the state and citizens, making it difficult for the police to prevent crime and maintain public order without resorting to force.

8. Consequences for policing and governance

When trust is low, police effectiveness declines because they lose access to vital information and community cooperation [1, 109]. Low trust also makes democratic governance less effective in general. Citizens who distrust the police are more likely to distrust other state institutions, including the judiciary and government. In fragile states, where police corruption, abuse, and brutality are more prevalent, the effect on public trust is even more explicit, making it difficult to establish stable and accountable institutions [44, 114].

Across Africa, the link between police misconduct and low trust is consistent; however, the strength of this relationship varies by country and context [9, 115]. In more stable states, such as South Africa, high levels of perceived corruption and brutality still correlate strongly with low trust, even if the institutional framework is relatively stronger [109]. In fragile states, where governance is weaker and accountability mechanisms are underdeveloped, the same levels of corruption and violence have an even more devastating effect on public confidence [44].

In both fragile and stable states or communities, however, the trend is distinct: Where police are perceived as corrupt, abusive, and brutal, public trust is usually low, and the morality of the police to enforce state laws is eroded [1, 2, 109]. Rebuilding trust, therefore, requires not only punishing individual officers but also systemic reforms to improve accountability, oversight, and community relations.

9. Restoring public trust in the police in Africa

Restoring public trust in the police in many African countries is a critical step towards addressing this complex challenge, considering the long history of corruption, abuse, and brutality perpetrated by law enforcement institutions. A plausible approach, therefore, would be for police authorities to adopt a multi-layered reform strategy that targets long-standing institutional or structural weaknesses, cultural issues, and accountability deficits, among others. It is anticipated that these strategies will help transform the institution and ultimately restore public confidence in the police.

10. Strengthening accountability and oversight

An important requirement for restoring public confidence in the police in many African countries is the establishment of vibrant, independent oversight bodies that are empowered to investigate misconduct by law enforcement agencies, particularly the police, in a transparent manner and enforce sanctions without any interference from the ruling political power, politicians, or other state agencies. When police officers are aware that they will be held accountable, the culture of impunity will diminish. Although countries like South Africa have oversight bodies in place, particularly the Independent Police Investigative Directorate (IPID), their effectiveness has often been hampered by limited resources and a lack of autonomy [116]. Nevertheless, other African countries can replicate such an initiative.

11. Police reform and professionalisation

Introducing vibrant reforms in the police force in many African countries will go a long way in reshaping police recruitment, prioritising candidates with community-oriented values and integrity over mediocrity. This can be achieved by raising educational qualification standards for recruits, enforcing compulsory periodic psychological screening for officers, and supporting vibrant compulsory training aimed at promoting human rights approaches to policing, ethics, and a non-violent approach to conflict resolution. For example, in Nigeria, some police reform initiatives were introduced following the #EndSARS movement, aimed at embedding community policing principles that emphasise building community trust rather than coercion [117, 118].

12. Promotion of community policing and community engagement

Building partnerships between police and communities in many African societies will not only shift policing from an abusive, brutal, or confrontational standpoint to a cooperative dynamic, but it will also engender or foster public confidence in the police. Across the globe, community policing and community engagement models have proven to facilitate intelligence gathering, enhance police responsiveness, and foster public trust by promoting police-citizen collaboration in social control and community-related crime decision-making, as well as cultivating mutual respect [119]. Research in Kenya and South Africa indicates that such models can reduce crime perception and increase confidence when genuinely implemented [120, 121].

13. Enhancing transparency and communication

A transparent complaint reporting system is pivotal for addressing incidents of police corruption, abuse, and brutality in Africa [56]. The establishment of a transparent complaint reporting system and functional hotlines is crucial. Online platforms should be established in communities to enable the public to report erring police officers promptly. This will also make the police, as an institution or organisation, more accessible and accountable. Such a transparent approach will boost confidence in the police and increase perceptions of police institutional fairness and legitimacy [122].

14. Institutional reforms

Institutional reforms are critical to addressing incidents of police corruption, abuse, and brutality. Institutional reforms are pivotal for improving not only working conditions for police officers but are also necessary for combating corruption, abuse, and brutality in many African societies [26, 43]. Reforms that aim to improve the salaries of police officers and establish incentive structures and motivations for prospective career progression paths will help discourage police officers' engagement in unethical practices, including abuse and brutality, as well as dependency on bribes and extortion [26, 43]. Such reforms will also empower police anti-corruption units with the necessary legal support to investigate corrupt officers.

15. Psychological support and welfare for officers

Providing psychological support and wellness programmes to challenged officers will help them manage work-related stress and reduce the likelihood of abusive behaviour stemming from frustration, burnout, or trauma [123]. Such a support system should not only cater to the psychological needs of officers, but it should also cover their welfare. It is believed that providing necessary welfare to police officers drastically reduces their likelihood of engaging in unethical practices [124].

16. Conclusion

Incidents of police corruption, abuse, and brutality in many African countries exemplify deep-rooted challenges that substantially erode public trust and confidence in law enforcement institutions. While many states' law enforcement institutions might have introduced reforms and other initiatives aimed at curbing these problems, the challenges have persisted. Such persistence reflects systemic weaknesses in law enforcement institutions, including poor or inadequate training, weak accountability mechanisms, institutionalised impunity, and sociopolitical and historical legacies of authoritarian governance. Such experiences not only undermine confidence in the police and the public they swore to protect but also, by extension, erode confidence in the legitimacy of democratic authorities in many African states.

As previously emphasised, addressing these problems requires vibrant reforms and other institutional measures. Such reforms involve raising educational qualification standards for recruits, enforcing compulsory periodic psychological screening for officers, and supporting vibrant compulsory training aimed at promoting human rights approaches to policing, ethics, and a non-violent approach to conflict resolution. The establishment of vibrant, independent oversight bodies will facilitate the investigation of misconduct cases involving law enforcement officials. It further requires the adoption and promotion of a partnership-building approach between police and communities. Police authorities also need to establish measures for enhancing transparency and communication. Providing psychological support and wellness programmes to challenged police officers is necessary. Fundamentally, sustained political will, combined with vibrant legal reforms that foster an independent judiciary and effective victim protection, must underpin any meaningful progress.

Ultimately, restoring public confidence in African police institutions requires more than technical fixes. It requires a transformational shift from a predatory policing approach toward a more civilised, human-rights-based approach to policing – a call to public service that is rooted in transparency, justice, and human rights. This drive is important not only for improving law and order but also for consolidating the legitimacy of democratic governance and social cohesion across the continent. Future focus can consider innovative ways to promote police accountability and support these transformations. By positioning police reforms within broader governance and societal frameworks, stakeholders in many African countries can find pragmatic and sustainable solutions to one of Africa's most pressing challenges facing the criminal justice system.

Author details

Paul Oluwatosin Bello[1]* and Adewale A. Olutola[2]

1 Faculty of Humanities, Independent Institute of Education, Roodepoort, South Africa

2 Department of Law, Safety and Security, Faculty of Humanities, Tshwane University of Technology, Pretoria, South Africa

*Address all correspondence to: pbello@iie.ac.za

References

[1] Bello PO. University students' accounts of police use of force: Implications for trust in the police. African Identities. 2024;**23**(3):634–652

[2] Bello PO. Do people still repose confidence in the police? Assessing the effects of public experience of police corruption in South Africa. African Identities. 2021;**19**(2):141–159

[3] Bello PO, John-Langba J. 'Are they truly our friends?' A preliminary evaluation of university students' confidence in the police. International Journal of Social Sciences and Humanity Studies. 2020;**12**(1):98–112

[4] Murphy K, Hinds L, Fleming J. Encouraging public cooperation and support for police. Policing & Society. 2008;**18**(2):136–155

[5] Malone MFT, Dammert L. The police and the public: Policing practices and public trust in Latin America. Policing & Society. 2021;**31**(4):418–433

[6] Maguire ER, Johnson D. Measuring public perceptions of the police. Policing: an International Journal of Police Strategies & Management. 2010;**33**(4):703–730

[7] Council HSR. Public Attitudes in Contemporary South Africa. Pretoria: HSRC Press; 2002

[8] Fry L. Trust of the police in South Africa: A research note. International Journal of Criminal Justice Sciences. 2013;**8**(1):36–46

[9] Olutola AA, Bello PO. An exploration of the factors associated with public trust in the South African Police Service. International Journal of Economics and Finance Studies. 2016;**8**(2):219–236

[10] Lekalake R. Law enforcers or law breakers?-Beyond corruption, Africans cite brutality. 2024

[11] Krönke M, Isbell T, Kakumba MR. Beyond corruption, Africans cite brutality and lack of professionalism among police failings. 2024

[12] Matthias Krönke TIMRK. Corrupt, brutal and unprofessional? Africa-wide survey of police finds diverging patterns. The Conversation. 2024

[13] Hope KR. Police corruption and the security challenge in Kenya. African Security. 2018;**11**(1):84–108

[14] Brecher JA. Rotten apple corruption. Encyclopedia of Criminal Justice Ethics. 2014

[15] Quick M. Bad apples or a rotten orchard: Detroit police culture and its protection of corruption. Rushton Journal of Undergraduate Humanities Research. 2024;**1**(1):6

[16] Gottschalk P, Dean G, Glomseth R. Police misconduct and crime: Bad apples or systems failure? Journal of Money Laundering Control. 2011;**15**(1):6–24

[17] Punch M. Police Corruption: Deviance, Accountability and Reform in Policing. Policing: A Journal of Policy and Practice; 2010;**4**(4):315–21

[18] Ivkovich SK, Sauerman A, Faull A, Meyer ME, Newham G. Police Integrity in South Africa. Routledge; 2020

[19] Haurovi M, Chilunjika A. Assessing the prevalence of unethical behaviour in the South African police service. Insights into Regional Development (Online). 2023;**5**(4):36–48

[20] Amagnya MA, Akinlabi OM, Bello PO. Police officers' assessments of factors that contribute to police corruption in Ghana. Policing: An International Journal. 2025;**48**(1):98–117

[21] Mkhwanazi ZM, Bello PO, Khosa D, Olutola AA. The marriage of convenience between the South African police service and the South African National Defence Force: The COVID-19 experience in the spectacle of national disaster. Acta Criminologica: African Journal of Criminology & Victimology. 2020;**33**(3):126–148

[22] Aborisade R, Fayemi J. Police corruption in Nigeria: A perspective on its nature and control. Nigerian Journal of Social Studies. 2015;**18**(2):245–262

[23] Oluwaniyi OO. Police and the institution of corruption in Nigeria. Policing & Society. 2011;**21**(1):67–83

[24] Dulani B, Asiamah GB, Zindikirani P. Amid rising corruption, most Africans say they risk retaliation if they speak up. 2023

[25] Sakpa D. In Africa, concerns over rising police brutality. Deutsche Welle. 2020

[26] Agbiboa DE. "Policing is not work: It is stealing by force": Corrupt policing and related abuses in everyday Nigeria. Africa Today. 2015;**62**(2):95–126

[27] Beek J, Göpfert M. Police violence in West Africa: Perpetrators' and ethnographers' dilemmas. Ethnography. 2013;**14**(4):477–500

[28] Hornberger J. Policing and Human Rights: The Meaning of Violence and Justice in the Everyday Policing of Johannesburg. Routledge; 2011

[29] Amusan L, Saka L. The Nigerian police force and the task of policing democratic Nigeria: Issues and problems. THE ANTHROPOLOGIST. 2018;**31**(1-3):105–116

[30] Makhofola FJM. The Escalating Police Brutality in Lesotho in Effecting Arrest Precipitated by Coalition Governments. National University of Lesotho, Faculty of Law; 2020

[31] Joseph N. A human rights analysis on Uganda police use of force in the execution of its roles. 2018

[32] Elechi OO. Extra-Judicial Killings in Nigeria. The Case of Afikpo Town. 2003

[33] Times T. How George Floyd died, and what happened next. The New York Times [Internet] Oct. Vol. **5**. 2021

[34] Roebuck JB, Barker T. A typology of police corruption. Social Problems. 1974;**21**(3):423–437

[35] Newham G. Strengthening democratic policing in South Africa through internal systems for officer control. South African Review of Sociology. 2005;**36**(2):160–177

[36] Mpako A, Ndoma S. South Africans' view of police marred by pervasive corruption, lack of professionalism. 2024

[37] Onyango G. The art of bribery! Analysis of police corruption at traffic

checkpoints and roadblocks in Kenya. International Review of Sociology. 2022;**32**(2):311–331

[38] Ulo E. "We give bribe to avoid delays": The dialectics of police-driver relations in Nigerian highways. Fuoye Journal of Criminology and Security Studies. 2024;**3**(1):194–212

[39] T. conversation. Corrupt, brutal and unprofessional? Africa-wide survey of police finds diverging patterns. 2024

[40] Vogl F. Waging War on Corruption: Inside the Movement Fighting the Abuse of Power. Bloomsbury Publishing PLC; 2012

[41] Faull A. Corruption in the South African police service: Civilian perceptions and experiences. Institute for Security Studies Papers. 2011;**2011**(226):24

[42] Andvig JC, Fjeldstad O-H. Crime, poverty and police corruption in developing countries. CMI Working Paper. 2008

[43] Hope KR. An analytical perspective on police corruption and police reforms in developing societies. Police Corruption and Police Reforms in Developing Societies. 2016;3–31

[44] Singh D. The causes of police corruption and working towards prevention in conflict-stricken states. Laws. 2022;**11**(5):69

[45] Famakin-Johnson OP. Police Brutality in the United States of America and Nigeria; A Comparative Analysis. Texas: Texas Southern University; 2022

[46] Agbiboa DE. They Eat Our Sweat: Transport Labor, Corruption, and Everyday Survival in Urban Nigeria. Oxford: Oxford University Press; 2022

[47] Mphidi AJ, Pheiffer DC. Corruption and moral degradation within the Tshwane Metropolitan Police Department. African Security Review. 2025;**34**(2):1–19

[48] Gillanders R, Ouedraogo I, Maïga WHE, Aja-Eke D. Police corruption and crime: Evidence from Africa. Governance. 2024;**37**(3):1015–1034

[49] Sokoni DW. Legal Aspects of Abuse of Police Powers in Tanzania. The Open University of Tanzania; 2024

[50] Nnadozie BC. Public Perceptions of Nigeria Police Monetary Bribery in Awka, Nigeria. Minnesota: Walden University; 2021

[51] Nyaoro D. Policing with prejudice: How policing exacerbates poverty among urban refugees. The International Journal of Human Rights. 2010;**14**(1):126–145

[52] Jonsson S. The complex relationship between police corruption and sex trafficking in origin countries. Journal of Human Trafficking. 2019;**5**(2):109–129

[53] Shaban SM. Examining Challenges Facing the Tanzania Police Force in Mitigating Illegal Immigrants: A Case Study of Bagamoyo District. The Open University of Tanzania; 2023

[54] Moran R. Contesting police credibility. Washington Law Review. 2018;**93**:1339

[55] Mbaku JM. Corruption in Africa: Causes, Consequences, and Cleanups. Lexington Books; 2007

[56] Faull A. Corruption and the South African police service. A review and its implications. Institute for Security Studies Papers. 2007;**2007**(150):20

[57] O'Hara P, Sainato VA. Monetizing the police: Corruption vectors in agency-managed off-duty work. Policy and Society. 2015;**34**(2):151–164

[58] Igba SA. Exploring the Role of Political Ethnicity on Police Use of Force in Nigeria: A Civil Society Perspective. South Africa: University of Pretoria; 2022

[59] Olutola A. The ruling political parties and the war against crime and corruption in Nigeria and South Africa: The case of two brothers with headless bodies. Acta Criminologica: African Journal of Criminology & Victimology. 2014;**27**(sed-2):81–95

[60] Alemika Etannibi EO. Police, policing and rule of law in transitional countries. In: Human rights and the police in transitional countries. Brill Nijhoff; 2003. p. 63–95

[61] Bello PO, John-Langba J. University students and police legitimacy: The South African Police Service before the loudspeaker. International Journal of Business and Management Studies. 2020;**12**(2):306–320

[62] Brand D. An Examination of the Approach to Police Reform from the Perspective of Serving Police Officers in the National Police Service of Kenya. Oxford: University of Oxford; 2023

[63] Bello PO, Matshaba TD. Procedural justice, police legitimacy, and performance: Perspectives of South African students. Journal of Psychology in Africa. 2021;**31**(1):43–48

[64] Waseem Z. A Postcolonial Condition of Policing? Decolonizing the Criminal Question: Colonial Legacies, Contemporary Problems. 2023;89–107

[65] Shadrack JT. Privatised Policing Duties in a Constitutional State: The Case of Postcolonial Tanzania in Socio-legal Context. Coventry: University of Warwick; 2020

[66] Oyakhirome IL. The Role of Social Activism in Pursuing Accountability for Police Abuse of Power in Africa. South Africa: University of Pretoria; 2024

[67] Vande PT, Letsuwa EM. Bad Governance, Citizens' Resistance and State Repression: A Study of the# EndSARS and# EndBadGovernance Protests in Nigeria. International Social Sciences and Education Journal. 2025;**3**(3):01–12

[68] Agbo HN, Ugwuanyi I. The politics of security agencies' control and election management in Nigeria. International Journal of Research in Arts and Social Sciences. 2019;**12**(1):188–201

[69] Idowu SS, Chukwudi EC. Police brutality and civil violence implications on societal peace and the economy: A study of end-Sars protests in Nigeria. Political Science and Security Studies Journal. 2021;**2**(3):3–15

[70] Iwuoha VC, Aniche ET. Protests and blood on the streets: Repressive state, police brutality and# EndSARS protest in Nigeria. Security Journal. 2021;**35**(4):1102

[71] Aniche ET, Iwuoha VC. Beyond police brutality: Interrogating the political, economic and social undercurrents of the# EndSARS protest in Nigeria. Journal of Asian and African Studies. 2023;**58**(8):1639–1655

[72] Bond P, Mottiar S. Movements, protests and a massacre in South Africa. Journal of Contemporary African Studies. 2013;**31**(2):283–302

[73] Alemika EE. Police practice and police research in Africa. Police Practice and Research: an International Journal. 2009;**10**(5-6):483–502

[74] Wairuri K. Beyond policy accountability: Responses to police abuse by people at Kenya's urban margins. 2022

[75] Lydia KW. The role of police in human rights abuse when effecting arrests in Kenya. 2013

[76] Kakumba MR, Krönke M. Brutality and Corruption Undermine Trust in Uganda's Police: Can Damage Be Undone? Afrobarometer; 2023

[77] Amanya N. A Critical Analysis of the Human Rights Perspective on The use of Force: A Case Study of the Uganda Police Force (Updf). 2017

[78] Okello A. Seychellois feel safe, but see police falling short of professional conduct. 2024

[79] Rashed D. Violence from above, violence from below: The state and policing citizens in Mubarak's Egypt. In: State Terror, State Violence: Global Perspectives. Springer; 2015. p. 93–113

[80] Nkrumah DO, Ofosuhene EY, Gyasi K. COVID-19 pandemic and presidential directives: The brutalities of the Ghana police service. Acta Criminologica: African Journal of Criminology & Victimology. 2020;**33**(3):1–27

[81] Wangari S, Priyanthi A. Survivors' perspectives: How to stay safe and struggle for justice'. Journal of the British Academy. 2022;**10**(s3):21–36

[82] Zondi Z, Ukpere W. Police brutality in post-apartheid South Africa reviewed. Mediterranean Journal of Social Sciences. 2014;**5**(3):574–579

[83] Gurr H, Oliver L, Harvey O, Subedi M, van Teijlingen E. The importance of positionality for qualitative researchers. Dhaulagiri Journal of Sociology and Anthropology. 2024;**18**(01):48–54

[84] Savin-Baden M, Major CH. Qualitative Research: The Essential Guide to Theory and Practice. London: Routledge; 2023

[85] Omale DJ. Police Ethics and Accountability: An Examination of Unethical Conducts and Corrupt Police Practices in Nigeria. In: Rethinking the Police for a Better Future: Navigating Policing Challenges with Accountability and Trust. Switzerland: Springer; 2025. p. 149–163

[86] Newham G, Faull A. Protector or predator? Tackling police corruption in South Africa. Institute for Security Studies Monographs. 2011;**2011**(182):65

[87] Berg J, Howell S. Civilian oversight of police in Africa: Trends and challenges. Civilian Oversight of Police: Advancing Accountability in Law Enforcement. 2016;121–138

[88] Masake PH. A Critical Assessment on Strategies to Detect and Combat Systemic Corruption in the Namibian Police Force. South Africa: University of South Africa; 2023

[89] Onyango G. Whistleblowing behaviours and anti-corruption approaches in public administration in

Kenya. Economic and Political Studies. 2021;**9**(2):230–254

[90] Okoye JN, Okafor N, Ojimba C. Corruption in the Nigerian public sector: Causes, consequences and sustainable solutions. International Journal of Advanced Multidisciplinary Research and Studies. 2024;**4**(5):1109–1117

[91] Akamike JO, Okonkwo ON, Ojima D. Effects of corrupt practices in the public sector: A case study of the Nigerian police service. African Journal of Social and Behavioural Sciences. 2023;**13**(2):567–581

[92] Olabiyi OM. The effect of bureaucratic corruption on household food insecurity: Evidence from Sub-Saharan Africa. Food Security. 2022;**14**(2):437–450

[93] Onyango G. Police Corruption at Traffic Checkpoints and Roadblocks in Kenya. In: Policing and the Rule of Law in Sub-Saharan Africa. London: Routledge; 2022. p. 31–49

[94] Hope Sr KR. Institutions and the culture dimension of corruption in Nigeria. Crime, Law and Social Change. 2018;**70**(4):503–523

[95] Ezeoha AE, Akinyoade A, Ehrhardt D, Uche C. Nigeria and the Practice of Whistleblowing–How Not to Mobilize Citizens' Participation in Anti-Corruption Programme. Public Integrity. 2025;1–21

[96] Osei-Adubofour K. The Lack of Political Impartiality of the Police in Ghana and Its Effect on the Public's Trust and Confidence in the Police and on Public Perception of Police Legitimacy. Boston: Northeastern University; 2017

[97] Baker B. Taking the Law into Their Own Hands: Lawless Law Enforcers in Africa. London: Routledge; 2017

[98] Sandhu A. 'I'm glad that was on camera': A case study of police officers' perceptions of cameras. Policing & Society. 2019;**29**(2):223–235

[99] Okukpon I, Eruaga OAO. Police brutality and human rights violations in the COVID-19 era through the lens of selected African Countries. ELTE Law Journal. 2021;23

[100] Annang A, Mensah RO, Adu-Adjei M, Asante E. The Prevalence of Crime Cases Involving Police Officers in a West African Country. Deviant Behavior. 2025;1–19

[101] Wanchinga MC. Knowledge and Utilization of Attitude Management in Interpersonal Conflicts among Police Graduates of Lilayi Training College in Lusaka Urban District. Lusaka: The University of Zambia; 2022

[102] Bello PO, Akinlabi OM, Amagnya MA. Satisfaction with the Police in South Africa: Perspectives of University Students. International Criminology. 2025;**5**(3):400–14

[103] Olutayo AA, Owoeye TP, Beatrice DA. Predators or protectors: Tales of Nigerian police force brutality on her youths. African Renaissance. 2025;**22**(2):285

[104] Bezuidenhout C, Kempen A. When the Protectors Become the Aggressors: Police Brutality in South Africa. In: Police Use of Force: Global Perspectives and Policy Implications. Springer; 2023. p. 267–287

[105] Bezie AE, Getachew Yenealem D, Asega Belay A, Bitew Abie A, Abebaw T,

Melaku C, Mamaye Y, Hailu Tesfaye A. Prevalence of work-related burnout and associated factors among police officers in central Gondar zone, Northwest Ethiopia, 2023. Frontiers in Public Health. 2024;**12**:1355625

[106] Sapanoi N. The Effects of Occupational Stress on Service Delivery in Zambia Police Service: A Case of Criminal Investigation Department (CID) in Lusaka Urban District. The University of Zambia; 2022

[107] Ugwuoke CO, Stephen MO, Ugwueze MI, Onah VC, Akwaji F. Police job stress, workload and burnout in Nigeria: The tired and frustrated cops. International Journal of Offender Therapy and Comparative Criminology. 2026;**70**(4):349–71

[108] Erasmus JJ. Community perceptions of South African Police Service responses to substance use and the impacts on health and well-being of community leaders and substance users in a peri-urban community in Cape Town. 2025

[109] Bello PO, Steyn J. Students'perceptions of the South African police service in durban, south africa: A non-judgmental assessment. International Journal of Social Sciences and Humanity Studies. 2019;**11** (2):61–85

[110] Agbiboa DE. Protectors or predators? The embedded problem of police corruption and deviance in Nigeria. Administration & Society. 2015;**47**(3):244–281

[111] Uslaner EM. Political trust, corruption, and inequality. In: Handbook on Political Trust. Edward Elgar Publishing; 2017. p. 302–315

[112] Gaichu JM, Onyango RSRDE, Odhiambo S. Influence Of Public Trust in the Police on Crime Reporting Behavior in Kamukunji Subcounty, Nairobi County, Kenya. 2024

[113] Olanrewaju SM. The Role of the Mass Media in the Fight against Police Brutality: A Case Study of The# EndSARS Protest in Nigeria. Chicago: Brac University; 2025

[114] Rothstein B. The Quality of Government: Corruption, Social Trust, and Inequality in International Perspective. University of Chicago Press; 2011

[115] Melkamu MT, Teshome W. Public trust in the police: Investigating the influence of police performance, procedural fairness, and police-community relations in Addis Ababa, Ethiopia. Cogent Social Sciences. 2023;**9**(1):2199559

[116] Vawda YA, Mtshali M. Who is watching the watchers?: A critical assessment of the Independent Police Investigative Directorate's prospects of investigating misconduct in the South African Police Service. Law, Democracy & Development. 2013;**17** (1):132–156

[117] Adeniyi E. 'We're now the walking dead': Predatory policing, youth agency and framing in Nigeria's# EndSARS social activism. African Studies. 2022;**81**(2):149–169

[118] Ezinna PC, Idoko CO, Nwogbo DC. The state and accountable policing: A diagnosis of# ENDSARS movement in Nigeria. Journal of Asian and African Studies. 2025;**60** (5):3136–3150

[119] Mohanty RK, Mohanty S. Community Policing as a Public Policy: Challenges and Recommendations. Cambridge Scholars Publishing; 2014

[120] Wanjohi DM. Influence of Community Policing on Crime Reduction in Kenya: A Case of Machakos County. University of Nairobi; 2014

[121] Dlamini S. Limited knowledge of community policing as a constraint to successful crime prevention: A case study of community members in Durban, South Africa. Acta Criminologica: African Journal of Criminology & Victimology. 2023;**36**(1):38–55

[122] Schafer JA. The role of trust and transparency in the pursuit of procedural and organisational justice. Journal of Policing, Intelligence and Counter Terrorism. 2013;**8**(2):131–143

[123] Stapleton KF. Breaking point: examining secondary traumatic stress, toxic leadership, coping mechanisms, and well-being in non-uniformed federal law enforcement personnel. 2025

[124] Blumberg DM, Papazoglou K, Creighton S. Bruised badges: The moral risks of police work and a call for officer wellness. International Journal of Emergency Mental Health and Human Resilience. 2018;**20**(2):1–14

Chapter 7

The Psychological Impact of Unjustified Police Suspicion

Tamar Hopkins

Abstract

Rather than the activity of a few 'bad apples' – policing without reasonable grounds – is a standard police practice with a psychological impact on policed people that deserves closer attention. This study examines the psychological consequences of being singled out by the police for suspicion. In particular, it examines the consequences of being singled out by police responding to a hunch rather than evidence of an offence. This study undertakes three separate analyses of the results of a survey of 981 Victorian Australians in 2018/2019 who were stopped by the police. Firstly, it quantitatively compares the differences in the psychological experience of people who have been stopped reactively, that is *with* reasonable justification, to the consequences for people who have been stopped *without* reasonable evidence of an offence. Using multinominal regression analysis, this study provides evidence that arbitrary, proactive vehicle stops cause greater psychological distress than vehicle stops where the reason for the stop is clearly apparent. Secondly, the study examines case studies from the survey, that illustrate how unjustified searches can be experienced as a form of discrimination. In the third section, through semi-structured interviews with survey recipients, the study reveals the ways proactive policing communicates the criminalised status of groups of racialised individuals and their communities in Australia and the psychological harm that this entails.

Keywords: pretextual stops, search powers, Victoria police, psychological harm, police contact, discrimination

1. Introduction

Police in Victoria, Australia have thousands of daily contacts with the public. While a proportion of this contact is public initiated, a considerable fraction is initiated by police. Police initiated stops can be divided into two types: proactive and reactive. Reactive stops are based on reasonable grounds and generally comply with legal limits on the use of police powers. Proactive stops involve police stopping an individual where no individualised objective justification exists. Proactive (or pretext) stops can be illegal, such as when police go beyond the authority of the legislatively conferred stop power to stop individuals for an ulterior purpose (see *The Queen v Gehan* [2019] NTSC 91) [1]. However, proactive stops can also be legislatively authorised. For example, police in Victoria have now been authorised to search individuals in designated areas for up to 6 months, without individualised reasonable suspicion (*Control of Weapons Act 1990* (Vic) 10D(3)(b)(ii)).

IntechOpen

Pretext stops and searches occur when police develop a hunch based on organisational rules about who to deem 'suspicious' [2, 3] rather than objectively justified reasonable suspicion of an offence. While police openly acknowledge the practice, [4] proactive vehicle stops are not authorised by Australian courts in the NT, NSW, SA and Qld for the purpose of criminal investigation [5]. Furthermore, because they breach human rights, legislation permitting proactive/pretext pedestrian searches is inconsistent with the *Charter of Human Rights and Responsibilities 2006* (Vic), and Australian's international human rights law obligations.

Victoria Police claim that the pretext search powers they have been granted by the Victorian Parliament have no negative consequences for innocent people: 'if you are not carrying a weapon then there is nothing to worry about' [6].

The overarching question this study seeks to answer is: Do innocent people in Victoria have nothing to worry about from unjustified police stops? What are the psychological consequences of being stopped by police and, in particular, when there is no objective justification? To explore these questions, this study undertakes a quantitative analysis of a survey of Victorians to examine the differences in people's experiences when they are stopped reactively (with reasonable justification) or proactively/pretextually (without individualised reasonable justification). It then examines a selection of police searches described by survey recipients to examine more deeply the subjective experience of being searched. Finally, it explores interviews with eight survey participants to investigate some key themes emerging in the data.[1]

2. What are some of the consequences of police contact?

International research indicates that police contact with the public can be criminogenic [7]. Police contact can increase law breaking behaviour and negative attitudes in young people [8] and can influence a person's life trajectory towards violent crime [9]. There is a relationship in highly disadvantaged communities between over-policing and increases in violent crime [10]. Rios found that in Oakland, Black and Latino youth resorted to crime as a form of resistance to the constant police attention, [11] while Cunneen [12] and Blagg [13] have made similar observations of resistance to police by Aboriginal youth in Australia. Research shows that racialised groups are more likely to experience police contact than their white peers.[2]

2.1 Psychological effects

International studies show that police stops can cause psychological harm to individuals who are stopped in numerous ways. Meares describes that the 'hidden agenda' of the criminal legal system is to teach people about their identity as citizens [15]. Tyler et al., note that police stops send a strong signal to individuals about their (lack of) worth and status in society.[3] Stops create shame, stigma and embarrassment [17]. Body searches can be experienced as a form of sexual violence.[4] Stops change people's decisions about the clothes they wear, where they go, who they go with and whether

[1] This research was approved by the UNSW Human Research Ethics Committee (Approval No. HC180500).

[2] [7, 14]

[3] [1, 16]

[4] [18]

they will drive.[5] The stopping and searching of newly arrived immigrants has been found to reduce people's attachment to and sense of belonging to their new country.[6] Police contact can lead to a decrease in homeless people's help seeking behaviours [21]. Furthermore studies have shown that police stops reduce people's engagement with local government and their participation in democratic life [22]. They reduce a person's likelihood of voting, [23] engagement with political life or capacity to act on their own political agency [22]. Police contact results in people withdrawing and retreating from public life. Lerman et al. explain:

> *Even when encounters are brief and do not lead to a poor outcome for the suspect, they can and do have a psychological impact that continues to exert its effect long after the encounter. Fagan, Tyler, and Meares (2011, 9) describe why: "being stopped by the government in a public space also suggests public discounting of worth. It appears to the person stopped to be a form of public shaming that derives from the feeling that the state has no problem displaying its power and control over the citizen on a public stage."*[7]

When people are subject to repeated police stops they stop trusting police.[8] They will not call the police if they are a victim of a crime, or if they witness a crime [24]. These international observations were replicated in Victoria in 2011, in the wake of a long-standing allegations of racial profiling [10]. Reflecting their distrust of local police, numerous members of the Flemington African community refused to assist police investigating the death of Ethiopian-Australian man Michael Atakelt preferring to make statements to a local community legal centre.[9] Similarly, following a high profile shooting in Sydney following widespread stop and search of the Lebanese community, community members refused to go to the police to give witness statements [25].

3. Methodology

The present study examines whether there is evidence in Victoria, Australia, that being singled out for unjustified police attention causes more harm to people than being subject to justified attention. It explores the emotional consequences of different types of police stops drawing from a survey. Firstly, it statistically analyses the responses people provide to a survey. Secondly, it examines a selection of examples of unjustified search descriptions provided by people answering the survey to draw out the emotional impact of such searches. Thirdly, drilling in deeper, it explores the impact of police stops on eight survey participants who agreed to participate in an interview.[10]

---

[5] Client stories related to me as a community lawyer also see [17]

[6] [19, 20]

[7] ([19, 20], 205).

[8] [16, 24]

[9] Personal experience.

[10] This research was approved by UNSW HREC–HC180500, participants provided their consent to being involved in research before commencing the survey questions. Participants who agreed to participate in an interview were asked to provide further written consent to participate.

3.1 Data collection and research design

In 2018, I constructed a 72 question online 'Police Stop Survey' and during 2018–2019, advertised an invitation to participate in the survey on the facebook sites of the Flemington and Kensington Community Legal Centre and the Victorian Aboriginal Legal Service in Victoria, Australia. I also distributed 1000 postcards to libraries and social services, inviting people to participate. In response to the invitation, 981 Victorians, 18 years and older, responded by describing their most recent experience of being stopped by police in vehicles or as pedestrians (for a fuller description see [26]).

3.1.1 Part 1. Variables

The key variable used in Part 1 of this study is 'stop type'. To create this variable I classified people's descriptions of their vehicle stop experiences into whether the police were exercising 'high', 'medium' or 'low' discretion when they stopped the person. I classified pedestrian stop experiences into three categories depending on whether the police had or had not claimed to have identified an offence before the stop occurred or whether they were speaking to the person as witness to an offence (This classification process is discussed in detail in Ref. [27]). For vehicle intercepts, high discretion stops are stops where the police, appear to the survey recipient, to have no objective justification on which to stop the person. Police either do not claim to justify these stops, or state they are a 'random intercepts'. These stops are indicative of pretextual/proactive policing. Medium discretion stops are stops involving the sighting of a minor offence before the stop occurs, such as a broken tail-light. These types of stops can also be used pro-actively where the minor infraction is used as a 'pretext' for a criminal investigation [1]. Low discretion stops occur when police stop someone because they observe a serious traffic offence such as going through a red light or where the police are testing batches of people for alcohol use without individual selectivity.[11]

The second key variable in this study is the person's emotional response to the stop. The survey asked respondents to select one or more of the feelings listed in **Table 1** to describe how they felt after this most recent experience of being stopped by the police. Where a person expressed a negative emotional feeling as a result of the police stop, it was classified as a 'negative emotional consequence'. Other feelings were classified as a 'positive or neutral emotional consequence'.

To undertake the statistical analysis, the study used multinomial regression analysis to produce an odds ratio of A. the odds of a person experiencing a high discretion stop compared with a low discretion stops against B. the odds of a person experiencing a negative emotional consequence compared to a neutral/position emotional consequence.[12]

For an additional analysis, survey respondents were asked if they thought the police were polite during the interaction, whether they thought the police were justified/reasonable during the interaction and their opinion of police at the end of the interaction. These opinions were not used to inform the classification of police stop type but were used to respond to an exploratory hypothesis on the effect of police politeness on people's opinions of police. Australian studies have shown that when police behave with greater procedural fairness, the psychological experience of the stopped individual

[11] See [27] for a full discussion of this methodology.

[12] Ref. [27].

Negative emotional consequence	Neutral or positive emotional consequence
Devalued	Not terribly bothered
Like i cannot go out without being stopped by the police/ under regular police surveillance	Satisfied with the police
Dehumanised/violated/humiliated	Accepting
Angry	Embarrassed but think the police were justified
Like i have no rights	Ok
That i was stopped because of my race/ethnicity/religion	Happy with police conduct
Stereotyped	Glad the police are around
Like a second-class citizen	That the police can generally be trusted to act within the law.
Scared/ fearful	
The police can get away with anything and there is nothing i can do about it.	

Table 1.
Emotional consequences – possible responses survey respondents could select following their description of a police stop.

is improved [16, 28]. Procedural fairness involves several components: trustworthiness, respectful treatment, neutrality and giving the stopped person a voice [28]. While potentially implicit within this framework, the concept of *substantive* fairness addresses a different issue. Substantive justice explores the legality or justification of the police action. In particular, the present study explores the emotional response of the individual who is singled out for unique attention where that attention does not appear to be justified. This permits an investigation of the effects of the substantive justice of the stop on the psychological experience of the stopped person.

3.1.2 Part 1. Statistical research hypotheses

To explore the impact of stop type on the emotional consequence for an individual, I constructed the following hypotheses:

A. Drivers stopped in high discretion intercepts (ie without objective justification) are more likely to experience negative emotional consequences as a result of the stop than drivers stopped for low discretion reasons.

B. When the stopped driver regards the police as polite, but also not justified in their conduct towards them, the driver will hold a negative opinion of the police.

C. Pedestrians and cyclists stopped before police claim that an offence has been identified are more likely to experience negative emotional consequences as a result of the stop than pedestrians/cyclists stopped after police claim an offence has been identified.

D. When the stopped pedestrian regards the police as polite, but also not justified in their conduct towards them, the pedestrian will hold a negative opinion of the police.

For research hypothesis A. and C., this study used multinomial logistical regression, controlling for age, gender, racial appearance, disability and LGBTQI status on multiply imputed data to create a, confidence interval and p-value (adjusted for multiple testing) of the ratio of the odds of experiencing a high discretion stop to a low discretion stop with the odds of a negative emotional outcome to a positive emotional outcome.[13] For pedestrians the odds ratio compared the number of no offence identified before the stop with offence identified with emotional outcome.

Research hypothesis B. and D. are exploratory only. This means the regression analysis does not utilise controls or multiple imputation to manage missing data. Furthermore, the p-values are not corrected for multiple testing. For this reason results for B. and D. need to be treated with greater caution than results for A. and C.

3.1.3 Part 2

To examine the impact of being searched without reasonable grounds, I selected four case studies from the survey that contained a sufficient description to investigate that person's response to what appeared to be an unjustified search. These case studies are not representative of the experiences of all people subject to a search without warrant, but rather provide a qualitative investigation into this experience. This method permits a qualitative exploration of the question, how do some individuals come to understand the experience of being singled out by police for a search in the absence of reasonable grounds?

3.1.4 Part 3

To explore more deeply the experience of being stopped, survey recipients were asked if they would agree to being interviewed. From those who agreed to participate, I selected two white people and six racialised people. My selection process maximised the racial diversity of the interviewees. Of the eight interviewees, seven gave me permission to seek their police stop history under the *Freedom of Information Act 1982* (Vic) ('FOI'). Through the semi-structured interviews I was able to explore qualitative examples of experiences of being stopped with and without reasonable grounds to highlight the differences and continuities in the psychological impacts of these stops. The method selected permits a qualitative exploration of the question, are there psychological implications for individuals when police single out an innocent individual for police investigation? The case studies use pseudonyms to protect the anonymity of the participants.

4. Results

4.1 Part 1

4.1.1 Vehicle stops

Of the stops recorded in the survey, 241 (50%) of people stopped by police in a vehicle were left with a negative emotional response, while 243 (50%) of people were left with a positive or neutral emotional responses. Interestingly no one chose feelings from both columns though it was open for them to do so.

[13] For a discussion the multiple imputation assumptions and methodology ([26], Chapter 6.)

Forty per cent of the vehicle stops described in the survey were low discretion stops. These stops involved clear traffic offences or stops at designated drug testing stations where drivers are pulled over in batches. In 17% of cases, police detected a minor offence before pulling a vehicle over. These are medium discretion stops. In 43% of cases described by survey recipients, police stopped individuals for high discretion reasons (routine/no reason intercepts or *random* preliminary breath testing).

Reading across **Table 2** you will observe that, consistent with hypothesis A, low discretion stops are associated with neutral or positive feelings while high discretion stops (pretext stops) are associated with negative emotional consequences. Medium discretion stops were also associated with negative feelings (**Table 2**).

The results of the multinomial regression analysis (**Table 3**) provide very strong evidence ($p < 0.001$, OR 2.31 [1.60, 3.35]) that being subject to a high discretion stop (ie random preliminary breath test or no reason/routine stop) is more likely to produce a negative emotional consequence for people compared with being stopped for low discretionary reasons (traffic safety, testing of batches at a designated stop station) controlling for race, disability, gender and LGBTIQ status. Overall 71.3% of racialised people experienced a negative emotional reaction following police contact while only 44% of white people experienced a negative response. However, I found no evidence of an interaction between race and stop type on people's emotional reaction to the stop. This means that stop type was a stronger predictor of negative emotional consequences than race.

4.1.1.1 *Impact of politeness in counteracting negative opinions of the police (vehicle stops)*

Forty-three people stopped by police in a vehicle found the police to be unreasonable but polite. Twenty-seven of those people left the encounter with a negative opinion of police, four with a positive view of police and 12 were not sure. Of the

Level of Discretion						
Emotional Consequence			Low	Medium	High	Total
	Neutral or positive	Count	139	30	74	241
		Column %	70.6%	35.3%	36.6%	49.8%
	Negative	Count	58	55	128	85
		Column %	29.4%	64.7%	63.4%	50.2%
	Total	Count	197	85	202	484
		Column %	100%	100%	100%	100%

Table 2.
Cross tabulation -emotional consequence by level of police discretion (vehicle stops).

	Reference group	P-value	Adjusted P-Value	Odds Ratio	Confidence interval
Odds of negative compared with positive/ neutral experience	High discretion stops compared with low discretion stops	<0.001	<0.001	2.31	1.60–3.35

Table 3.
Multinomial regression – emotional experience by stop type (vehicle stops).

people who thought the police behaved politely, the exploratory analysis revealed that when they also view the police as unreasonable, they formed negative opinion of police at the end of the stop ($p < 0.001$, OR 31.52 [9.25–107.45]).

4.1.2 Pedestrian/bicycle stops

In the following section, 'pedestrian' refers to pedestrian and bicycle stops. Using the same variable coding system reported in **Table 1**, 55% of people stopped as pedestrians reported negative emotional consequences because of the stop (57/103). Overall, 71.4% of racialised pedestrians and 51.2% of white pedestrians had a negative emotional response to the stop (**Table 4**).

Reading across **Table 5**, you will observe that regardless of the whether the police provided a reason or not for the stop, 60% or more people who were stopped as pedestrians in the sample, suffered from negative emotional consequences following their encounter with the police. That is, they experienced feelings of fear, anger, humiliation or degradation because of their encounter. Those stopped for no reason, in my sample, had a slightly more negative emotional response to the police. Those stopped as a witness to an offence were 100% positive or neutral about their feelings about the police.

To determine the statistical significance of these associations, I performed a multinominal logistical regression, controlling for age, gender, racial appearance, disability and LGBTQI status on multiply imputed data.[14]

The regression analysis produced no evidence that the police reason for stopping an individual had an impact on the emotional experience of those subject to pedestrian stops.

4.1.2.1 Impact of politeness in counteracting negative opinions of the police (pedestrian stops)

Forty-six pedestrians thought the police were polite but unreasonable. Twenty-nine of these people left the interaction with a negative opinion of the police while 5

	Stop Type					
Emotional Consequences			**Witness to an offence**	**Offence alleged**	**No Offence alleged**	**Total**
	Positive/ Neutral	Count	12	12	20	57
		Column %	100%	40%	33%	
	Negative	Count	0	18	39	44
		Column %	0%	60%	66%	
	Total	Count	12	30	59	101
		Column %	100%	100%	100%	100%

Table 4.
Crosstabulation – emotional consequences by stop type (pedestrians).

[14] For a discussion the multiple imputation assumptions and methodology ([26], Chapter 6).

Stops Types	Reference Group	P-Value	Odds Ratio	Confidence	Interval	Adjusted P-Value
Negative v Positive/ Neutral emotional consequence	No offence v offence-based stops	0.335	1.682	0.532	5.317	1

Table 5.
Multinomial regression – odds ratios of emotional consequences by stop types (pedestrians).

had a positive opinion of police at the end of the interaction. The exploratory findings revealed that of the pedestrians who thought police were polite, those who also viewed the police as unreasonable were much more likely ($p < 0.001$) to have a poor opinion of police at the end of the stop: OR 16.51 [5.28–51.63].

4.2 Part 2: Understanding the experience of being subject to an unjustified police search

To understand why the experience of being investigated for criminality in the absence of reasonable grounds might be psychological harmful, I examine four of the descriptions people provided in the survey of their experience of being searched in the absence of reasonable grounds for suspicion (**Figure 1**).

Case 679 involves an Aboriginal man, forced to submit to the search of his car without justification. He is left feeling devalued, racially stereotyped and like he has no rights. Being treated as suspicious by police is an uncomfortable experience. However this man's experience indicates that, for him, when it is done without a rational basis, it undermines his sense of fairness and justice. It leaves him feeling powerless, unable to protect himself from present or future interference.

Reason for the stop? They wanted to search my car, they said it was a random search.
What did they do? They pulled me out of the car, searched my car and checked my license then asked me about what I was up to and whose car it was.
What happened in the end? Free to go.
Felt that the police were: unjustified, unprofessional, racially motivated.
He feels: devalued, stereotyped, like he has no rights and that he's under constant police scrutiny.
Why did you answer the police questions? Because they said if I didn't answer the questions, I could be arrested
Why didn't you make a complaint? I didn't think anyone would listen or take me seriously.

Figure 1.
Case 679 Aboriginal man – No reason, investigative stop, September 2018 Melbourne CBD [26].

The next vehicle search case leaves the person feeling angry, like they have no rights and that the police can get away with anything and there is nothing they can do about it. The person's explanation for the search is that they were on route to a music festival. Being on route to a music festival does not provide reasonable grounds to suspect that a person has drugs, but like racial appearance, provides an (unlawful) basis for the otherwise arbitrary policing (**Figure 2**).

Case 906

Why did the police stop you? breath test and drug test (was on route to a music festival)
What happened? Breath test and license check. Then walked a sniffer dog around the car. Dog didn't indicate anything. Then asked if I could open doors to let the dog sniff inside the car. When I refused they tried to convince me. When I still refused they said they had reason to suspect I had drugs in the car and directed me to pull over for them to search the car. They searched the car and found nothing. When queried, they said refusing to open the doors was reasonable grounds to search the car. Which I disagree with.
How did you feel? Angry, like I have no rights, that the police can get away with anything and there is nothing I can do about it.
Why didn't you complain? I didn't feel it would change anything. Also I do research into policing and it could jeopardise my research

Figure 2.
Case 906 [26].

In the next case, the passenger feels stereotyped, like he had no rights and that the police could get away within anything and there was nothing he could do about it. Again, his explanation for the search is that the person is on route to a music festival (**Figure 3**).

Case 880 Muslim/Middle Eastern passenger, White driver

Why did the police stop the car? To check for drugs. They were profiling vehicles and ushering the ones they thought that looked suspiciously simply because we appeared to be going to a festival. Mere suspicion of going to a festival isn't a crime, and the assumption that if you are going to a music festival then you'll do drugs is unreasonable.
What happened? An officer ushered the car into an area where they were conducting different types of searches that was off the main road. An officer approached the driver as the driver rolled down the window. They asked them questions about what we were doing and if there were drugs in the vehicle. They asked if they could use a sniffer dog for the outside of the car. The driver said that they did not consent but if the police had the power to then there would be nothing they could do to stop them. The police brought a sniffer dog to the car and got it to sniff the exterior or the car and in particular nooks and crannies. The officer said that the dog had detected drugs and informed us that they wanted to search the inside of the car. The driver disputed whether the dog had given the police the indication that the dog had sniffed drugs. The police directed the driver to park the car a few metres away, but still in the compound, so that it could be searched. The car, our things, and we were searched. They gave me and the driver a pat down search. They found nothing and let us go.

Figure 3.
Case 880 [26].

In case 880, the driver is certain that the real basis for the police search is that they are on route to a music festival. Like race, this provides an (unlawful) basis for the otherwise inexplicable police conduct.

This kind of policing is not unusual. On 9 December 2019, shortly after the survey closed, *the Age* reported on an operation where police stopped and searched 340 vehicles going into a festival [29]. It is highly unlikely police had reasonable grounds to suspect the presence of drugs in every case.

The next case study provides evidence that the negative impacts of high discretion policing is not necessarily ameliorated by the fact that the policing is *lawful*. Below is an example of a lawful search of a pedestrian in designated areas under the *Control of Weapon Act 1990* (Vic). As stated above, in Victoria, police can search people for weapons inside a designated area without reasonable grounds (**Figure 4**).

Case 874 non-binary white person

Why were you stopped by police? searching people inside a weapons search area in the CBD in October 2018.
What happened next? continued to search other people in the weapons search area
How did they treat you? I was pushed, nothing heavier than that.
How were the police? Politically motivated, homophobic, transphobic, rude, aggressive, disrespectful, unprofessional.
I felt: Angry, like I have no rights, like police can get away with anything and there is nothing I can do, scared and fearful.
Why didn't you complain? Complaints are barely taken anywhere and cops investigating cops is a fucking joke.

Figure 4.
Case 874 [26].

Despite its legality, this high discretion, investigative search leaves the person feeling that the search was politically motivated and trans/homophobic. Even when the legislature makes suspicion-less stop and searches legal, this example shows they can be experienced as abusive and illegitimate by the stopped person. Importantly, here, legality is less critical than reasonable justification.

4.3 Part 3: Interviews

Eight interviewees detailed six pedestrian stops, three bicycle stops and ten vehicle stops in Victoria. In 11 of the 19 stops, police had observed the person committing an offence before they stopped the person. In eight of the 19 stops, police used unjustified post-stop conduct. People's names have been altered to protect anonymity.

Table 6 describes six racialised and two white people's descriptions of 19 police stops reported during an hour-long interview. People's reactions to the police stops

	Stop	Justification	Impact	Vic Pol reason (FOI)[a]	Classification
Abel Indian/ Hispanic background	Pedestrian Stop 1	Jaywalking	Thinks jaywalking in safe conditions should not be a crime	Walking across a road on a flashing red light	Offence Observed Justified post-stop conduct
	Pedestrian Stop 2	Drunk in public	Concerned about the criminalisation of public drunkenness	Drunk in Public	Offence Observed Justified post stop conduct
Bai Chinese background	Cyclist Stop 1	Riding without a helmet	Frustrated that riding without a helmet is a crime	—	Offence observed Justified post stop conduct
	Cyclist Stop 2	Riding without a helmet	Frustrated that riding without a helmet is a crime	—	Offence observed Justified post stop conduct
Dana Hispanic	Pedestrian Stop 1	Allegedly drunk in public	Large psychological impact, potential PTSD	No authority to seek police records provided.	Offence allegedly observed, Unjustified post stop conduct

	Stop	Justification	Impact	Vic Pol reason (FOI)[a]	Classification
Effram Ethiopian	Pedestrian Stop 1	No reason	Left feeling powerless	—	No offence observed Unjustified post-stop conduct
	Cyclist Stop 2	Not wearing a helmet	Left feeling distrustful	—	Offence observed Justified post stop conduct
	Vehicle Stop 3	No reason	Powerless, distressed	—	High discretion, Unjustified post-stop conduct
	Pedestrian Stop 4	No reason	Frustrated, distressed		No offence observed, Unjustified post-stop conduct
	Pedestrian Stop 5	No reason	Racially profiled, Angry	—	No offence observed, unjustified post stop conduct
	Vehicle Stop 6	No reason	Racially profiled, Angry.	—	High discretion, unjustified post stop conduct
	Vehicle Stop 7	No reason[b]	Angry, Racially profiled	—	High discretion, unjustified post-stop conduct.
Ghatala Muslim	Vehicle Stop 1	Using a mobile phone	Initial frustration at receiving a fine and concern that had been racially profiling. But accepting.	—	Offence observed Justified post stop conduct
Hondo African	Vehicle Stop 1	Unregistered car	Accepting	—	Low discretion, unjustified post stop conduct.
	Vehicle Stop 2	No reason	Angry, Racial profiled	—	High discretion, unjustified post stop conduct.
Colin Anglo/Dutch	Vehicle Stop 1	Random	No impact	—	High discretion stop Justified post stop conduct[c]
	Vehicle Stop 2	Using a mobile phone	No impact, not fined.	—	Offence observed Justified post stop conduct
Fred Anglo/Irish	Vehicle Stop 1	Red light	No impact	—	Low discretion, justified post stop conduct.
	Vehicle Stop 2	Seatbelt	A bit annoyed by the fine.	—	Medium discretion, justified post stop conduct.

[a]*Police records existed only for two of the 19 stops described by the 8 individuals.*
[b]*Victoria Police policy states that speed offences should be strictly enforced, and further all drivers be subject to a PBT. In this case no fine was issued, nor was Effram subject to a PBT, indicating the police were motivated to find out if he had committed a non-apparent criminal offence (an investigate stop) rather than to perform a traffic safety stop.*
[c]*While this is a high discretion stop, it is not a proactive stop because the police did not go on to question or search him. The stop remained focussed on the legal stop reason.*

Table 6.
Summary of stops described by interviewees [26].

depended on several issues: their views on the reasonableness of the initial stop, whether they agree with the law being enforced, and whether they consider the police post-stop conduct to be justified. Those from 'targeted racialised' groups[15] (Aboriginal, Pasifika, African, Middle-Eastern/Muslim) were more aware of the impact of their racial appearance on the police than people from other racialised groups.

Abel who is gay and part Indian, part Anglo-Saxon and part Portuguese, describes two stops, a jaywalking incident and a drunk in public incident. In the first stop, Abel believes that the police should not have wasted their time issuing a fine to him for jaywalking in a safe setting. In the second stop, Abel is concerned about the criminalisation of drunkenness, but does not dispute the facts. The police drove him from a train station to his cousin's place and then fined him. In neither case did he question the factual circumstances behind the stop basis. These were factually justified stops, but in the first stop, Abel thinks the police discretion should have been exercised to caution him. Abel does not believe his racial appearance had any impact on the police decision-making, however he thinks that a straight man may have been able to convince the police not to pursue the jaywalking charge. Abel is angry about the police conduct in the jaywalking case. Abel is not upset with the police in the public drunkenness case, but would like public drunkenness to be decriminalised so that it is no longer the police role to respond.[16]

Bai (who is of Chinese appearance) was stopped twice for riding a bike without a helmet. In both cases he's angry and frustrated, not with the police (they stopped but did not fine him) but the government for imposing a law on him that requires him to wear a helmet. He has thoroughly researched the facts around the safety issues and inhibitory effects of helmet laws and is part of a group actively seeking law reform. He does not believe his racial appearance had any impact on the police decision-making.

Both Abel and Bai's cases provide evidence that that when police have a legal basis to stop a person based on that person's *illegal behaviour*, even if the stopped person does not agree with the law, racialised people will not necessarily believe their race played a role in police decision-making. Neither of these people experienced unjustified post-stop conduct. They are frustrated with the laws, not the police. This contrasts with the next case study, where the factual basis for the arrest is disputed.

Dana, a young Hispanic woman was also stopped for public drunkenness. Dana was not drunk when she was stopped by the police. For her, both the police decision to stop her and their post-stop conduct was unnecessary and excessively punitive and violent. Interestingly, while she could have, Dana did not view her experience from a racial perspective: she experienced it as misogynist. Dana was stopped for being drunk in public, while walking and looking at a map on her phone to find a party. Because her attention was focused on her phone, she guesses she may have missed the first call the police made from their vehicle while driving passed to get her attention. She thinks that because she did not react to their first call for her attention, the police became angry and thought she was ignoring them. On contact, the police immediately handcuffed and pushed her to the ground, causing her dress to ride up. She felt degraded and distressed. A concerned passer-by phoned her boyfriend who arrived and asked to take her home. Then, unlike Abel's experience above where the police drove him to his cousin's home, Dana was detained and driven to the police station. On her way to the police station Dana was

[15] This characterisation is defined in [26].

[16] Since this interview, public drunkenness has been decriminalised in Victoria and is now responded to as a public health issue by Co-health.

injured in the back of the police divvy van because of the violent swerves of the divvy van. At the police station, a police officer asked Dana if he could take a personal photo of her. While Dana was eventually released, this humiliating, degrading and injurious experience has left Dana unwilling to leave the house at night and she continues to experience flashbacks. Dana appears to be suffering long term psychological injuries but is too fearful to make an official complaint or take civil action.

Effram, who is of Ethiopian origin and appearance, described seven police stops in Victoria during his interview, six of which appear to have had no clear basis to justify the police decision to stop him. The frequency with which Effram had been subject to unjustified policing contrasted sharply with other interviewees. Effram was acutely aware that he was subject to more scrutiny by police than white people. On one occasion, Effram was searched while his white friends were not. On the one occasion Effram was stopped for a reasonable justification, he was charged for not wearing a helmet while his white friends were not. In other cases there was no direct comparator to allow him to observe the difference in treatment, however the frequency of the unjustified suspicion and degrading treatment provides insight into its racialised nature. In one case, when he was a child, a police officer drove up onto the footpath next to him and demanded his complete compliance in answering questions before driving away. On another occasion he was investigated after smiling at an officer and followed home. Another time he was questioned whilst carrying a TV on a street. The police were not investigating a theft, but thought Effram should be questioned about where he got his TV from.

Hondo of Zimbabwean origin experienced two police stops. The first occurred when he was a passenger in an unregistered vehicle driven by another man of African appearance. He recounts that when the police stopped the car, they said, "Get the fuck out of the car" to the two young black men and told them to kneel on in the gutter. Hondo feels like the police were justified in treating him this way and is angry with his friend for driving an unregistered car. It was the second stop Hondo experienced that has upset him. He was pulled over while driving in Melbourne's eastern suburbs and had his visa status checked in circumstances where this was not happening to white people. The clear racially discriminatory treatment he experienced during this second stop has left him deeply angry and disturbed. Hondo's acceptance of the police treatment of him in the first stop is also disturbing to me. He describes being degraded and humiliated, but he has rationalised it as acceptable conduct because the car he was in was unregistered. My survey results show however, that police stop unregistered cars all the time *without* behaving in an aggressive and humiliating manner.

Ghatala, an Iranian Muslim women who wears a hijab, states that because the legislature has created laws (she described the anti-terrorism laws) that are used to target Muslims, her first instinct is to distrust the police. She explains that racist, unjustified policing experienced either individually or by members of her community leave people fearful about standing up for themselves and their community. While Ghatala did eventually accept the fairness of a medium discretion police- stop she encountered (she was stopped for using a mobile phone while driving) she was certain the police had identified her headscarf first before exploring whether she had committed an offence. The interview with Ghatala and the other racialised interviewees revealed that they do not call the police when they are the victim of a crime and they do not make complaints. They each describe using strategies to resolve issues themselves rather than relying on Australia's dispute resolution institutions.

In my interviews with the two white straight men, I observed that both men saw police as people who could be reasoned with. One was able to negotiate his way out of a fine and the other was able to evade, on several occasions, being subjected to a search despite being in possession of illegal drugs. Both white interviewees provide evidence of being able to elicit police sympathy or comradery. This was not the experience of the racialised interviewees. Bai (of Chinese appearance) managed to evade fines for riding without a helmet, but not through eliciting sympathy: but by asking police to investigate another offence. Charging him may have involved the police in more work than they were willing to do. This ended up being an effective fine avoidance strategy.

5. Discussion

5.1 Limitations of the study and validity of findings

This study utilised a convenience sample of people who responded to an invitation to participate and is not a random sample of the Victorian population. It is necessarily biased through participant self-selection and through the locations of where the invitation to participate were advertised. Consequently, the frequencies of different stop types experienced by respondents cannot be extrapolated to the general population. Neither can the frequencies of emotional response to being stopped be extrapolated to the general population. However, if, as the police presume, people are not negatively emotionally impacted when they are subject to a 'random' (that is high discretion) vehicle stop or a pedestrian stops where there is no claim of evidence of offending, then we would expect to see no positive relationship between 'high discretion' vehicle stop or 'no offence' observed pedestrian stop types and negative emotional responses within this data set. Responses to the survey indicated that people reported an even distribution between positive/neutral and negative emotional outcomes arising from their stop experience. Because this study involves a comparison of emotional responses to different stop types within a similarly biased cohort of responders, evidence of a pattern of responses will be suggestive that a relationship between stop type and emotional response exists.

This study relies on descriptions provided by members of the public to determine the level of police discretion involved in their stop. Because members of the public may not be aware of the full circumstances of a stop when they describe them, their conclusions will necessarily involve errors. However, because this issue impacts all descriptions, this study's findings, which, in Part 1 are based on a internal comparison of similarly error-proned civilian descriptions remain valid. This internal comparison is of sufficient value to explore a claim that the singling out of individuals, where no reasonable grounds exists, for investigation carries no negative emotional consequences.

The selection of case studies in both Part 2 and 3 was not random. Part 2 permitted an inquiry into the experiences of some individuals who have been searched without reasonable grounds. In Part 3, cases were chosen to deliberately increase the number of interviews with racialised survey participants who agreed to participate. While this self-selection process will involve biases and may include people who have stronger opinions about the police than others, these accounts are nonetheless capable of evidencing real experiences to assess whether innocent individuals have nothing to worry about from proactive policing.

5.2 Part 1 statistical analysis

The results of Part 1 provide strong evidence that people stopped for no reason in vehicle stops compared to a clear traffic safety reason have 2.3 times the odds ($p < 0.001$, OR 2.31 [1.60, 3.35]) of experiencing negative psychological consequences as a result of the stop compared to a positive or neutral psychological experience. The study found no evidence of an independent interaction between race and negative emotions. The absence of evidence that being subject to a high discretion vehicle stop interacts with minority status on people's emotional experience provides an alternative perspective to studies that find racial minorities are more likely to come to negative conclusions about police conduct than others [30]. The present finding provide evidence that a person's emotional response to a vehicle stop is correlated to whether the police initial reason to stop them was reasonably justified. This points to the conclusion that improving people's opinions of police lies not so much in improving community police relations, but through improving the reasonableness of individual police intervention decisions.

The results also provide an indication that reasonableness in the basis for the police stop, may be more important to people's opinion of police than police politeness. While this does not eliminate the need for police politeness, it sends a clear signal to police agencies they must focus on ensuring police possess an objectively reasonable justification before they stop and subsequently engage with people.

5.2.1 Comparison of vehicle and pedestrian/bicycle stops

This study found no evidence that stop reason effects the type of emotional response a person will have to being stopped by police as a pedestrian or cyclist. An explanation this arises from the discovery that overall pedestrian stops were experienced by stopped individuals as more controversial and contested than vehicle stops ([26], Chapter 4). For example, most people, who answered the survey, who were stopped for being drunk in public or drinking in a restricted zone disagreed that they were drinking and were, in fact, free to go at the end of the encounter (9 of 14 people stopped for these reasons were free to go at the end of the encounter) [26]. In these cases, police have provided the person with a reason for the stop, thus resulting in a their classification for the purpose of this study as 'offence identified' stops, but the person disagrees with the police assessment. This disagreement is likely to have provoked strongly negative feelings despite the police claiming to have identified a particular offence before they stopped the individuals. Similarly, those stopped for failing to wear a helmet were frustrated with the helmet laws themselves as well as inconsistencies with the police enforcement of those laws which provoked a negative emotional response in them, despite the police having a legitimate reason to stop the person. All of these stops were classified as 'offence observed'. Their responses contrast sharply with drivers who were stopped on the basis that the police had observed an offence. Drivers stopped because police had identified an offence were much more accepting of police intervention. These results indicate that the enforcement of traffic laws where offences are detected before the stop or where stops are carried out on batches of individuals with no opportunity for police selectivity are less controversial than the enforcement of laws impacting pedestrians and cyclists. The results also suggest that future studies should rethink the classification of pedestrian stop types.

For both vehicle stops and pedestrian stops, the data suggests that police politeness does not improve the opinion of a person about the police if they believe the stop is unreasonable. These results indicate that being polite will not ameliorate the poor opinion of police induced in a person subject to an unreasonable or unlawful police stop. While procedural justice is more than mere politeness, these results put substantive justice in the spotlight for attention by police agencies. From these results we can speculate that civilian experiences of policing could be improved by ensuring police possess a reasonable and objective justification before they stop and investigate a person.

These results indicate that people's experience of being stopped by police cannot be assumed to be psychological neutral, even if they are innocent. Most pedestrian and bicycle stops were experienced as psychologically harmful, while for vehicle stops the psychological harm was greater when the stop was a pretextual: without reasonable grounds. This provides evidence to legislatures that police-initiated contact, involving the singling out of an individual, should only be lawful when there are objectively reasonable grounds to permit an interference with a person's fundamental human rights to privacy, and freedom of movement and freedom from arbitrary detention.

5.3 Part 2: Experiences of unjustified searches

The examination of the police search cases reveals something important. The absence of a reasonable basis for suspicion for the police treatment (even if the treatment is legal) led the searched person to conclude that the police were either politically motivated, racist, homophobic, transphobic or a combination of one of these. This indicates that when suspicion-less police searches are made legal, this is likely to lead to an increase in people's distrust of the police.

The explanation people believed to be the real reason behind the police decision for the search was their racial or gender/sexual identity or their presence at a protest or travel to a music festival. This is consistent with the observation of policing scholars, that arbitrary police powers are used to control racial and sexual 'deviants' and outgroups such as those who attend 'disorderly' events [18, 31–33].

In one of the case studies, the police search of an Aboriginal man in the absence of reasonable grounds felt racially motivated. This man's perception that the police were racially motivated has a rational basis for (at least) three reasons. The police decision to search him, in particular, was unlikely to be truly random. In this case, based on the information we have, there was no reason, other than race, that explains the police decision to select him for a 'random' search. Secondly, there is strong evidence that police *do* subject Aboriginal, African, Middle Eastern and Pasifika drivers to unjustified post stop investigation much greater odds than white people in Victoria [26]. Thirdly there is a history of over-policing of Aboriginal people by police in Australia [34]. In the absence of a reasonable explanation for the search, racial profiling is a reasonable conclusion to draw.

The case study of the unjustified search of the individual who was in a designated search area, illustrates that when police are provided with powers to search without individual justification, their actions can be experienced as discriminatory. Furthermore, without a justification requirement, a clear risk exists that police will act, consciously or otherwise on their biases.

These cases reveal the cost to people of being subject to searches without objective justification. People are left feeling dehumanised, angry, devalued and scared. Furthermore they feel powerless: subject to illegal or unjustified policing with no avenue for redress. Importantly, in the absence of rational explanation, searches are experienced as discriminatory.

5.4 Part 3: Interviews

Effram and Hondo's long form interviews permit a close look at the experience of being singled out, without reasonable grounds, for people whose racial group is subject to racial profiling [27]. Both Effram and Hondo describe that feeling singled out for police attention where race appears to be the explanation, can have had far reaching, long-term impacts on their feelings about themselves, their safety, and fears about being further criminalised by the police. They also expressed feelings of powerlessness that extend beyond their individual experience with the police. They describe that both individually and as a community, their complaints against racist policing have gone nowhere. For both Effram and Hondo, the policing re-enforced their perception of their immigrant status as being tenuous and fragile. They feel that they will never belong and that they are perpetually suspicious. Hondo fears receiving death threats if he spoke up about the racism he experiences. Effram describes his whole community as being deeply distrustful and disillusioned with police. Now that Effam has children, he is seriously considering leaving Australia to protect them from the policing he experienced. Effram observes that for police, racism is "so normal it's like drinking water."

These accounts provide clear examples that unjustified police contact has detrimental consequences. Importantly, it reveals that innocent people can be seriously harmed by police stops. Dana, Effram and Hondo, were each stopped while innocent in at least one of their stops and have each been left with strongly negative psychological outcomes as a consequence of those stops. Furthermore, each experienced the unjustified police conduct as either racist or misogynist (ie discriminatory). These accounts reveal the serious psychological harm involved when police stop innocent people without objectively reasonable grounds to suspect an offence has occurred.

6. Conclusion

The three methods used in this study have revealed that unjustified stops and/or searches in Victoria can result in psychological harm to innocent individuals. This rebuts the police claim that innocent people have nothing to worry about. Firstly, the survey data reveals that the odds of a motorist feeling scared, fearful, degraded, humiliated or stereotyped by police is 2.3 times the odds ($p < 0.001$, OR 2.31 [1.60, 3.35]) for drivers stopped for no reason that for drivers stop where reasonable justification exists. While method one produced no findings on stop type differences in psychological experiences for pedestrians, this is likely to be because, many pedestrian stops are not experienced as legitimate, even when a stop reason is provided by police.

The exploratory results find that experiencing unjustified policing reduces a person's opinion of police and that this opinion is not improved by the police acting politely. These findings provide evidence that police politeness (a form a procedural fairness) does not ameliorate the emotional impact of the substantive unfairness that occurs when the police engage in unreasonable or unjustified conduct. An unjustified but polite search does not neutralise the harmful impact of police conduct that has no objective basis. This confirms that objective justification is an important factor in people's opinions of the police.

Evidence from the second analysis: an examination of case studies of searches, indicates that where there is no justification for police searches, people may characterise the police as homophobic, racially motivated, or unfairly targeted at categories of people such as music festival goers or protesters. This indicates that searches without reasonable grounds are experienced as biased and discriminatory.

Method three - the interviews - provide evidence that unjustified policing can have long standing impacts. Unjustified stops, and a lack of accountability for them, leave people feeling discriminated against with no recourse. Stops that are experienced as discriminatory result in people losing faith in the justice system. Furthermore, constant experiences of being singled out for investigation, in the context of a similar experiences across a whole community decreases trust and belonging. Unjustified policing conveys powerful messages: you do not belong, you do not matter, you are powerless, you will not be believed. Furthermore, these powerful messages are conveyed directly from the actions and words of the State's representatives. Critically, unjustified experiences, are experienced as discrimination.

These findings question claims that everyday pro-active, pretextual police activities do not harm innocent people. They add to the growing evidence base that policing without reasonable grounds for suspicion is not just arbitrary and ineffective at identifying crime, but harmful. While policing based on reasonable suspicion can be unpleasant, the unnecessary intrusion of unjustified policing causes more distress and re-enforces the racial stratification of Australian society. For example, Hondo has come to terms with the aggressive policing he experienced when the car he was in was unregistered but continues to be deeply impacted from being singled out for questioning when there was no basis to stop him. This finding sharply contradicts police claims in Victoria that if you are innocent, you have nothing to worry about.

Acknowledgements

Thank you to Vicki Sentas and Gordana Popovic.

Conflict of interest

The author declares no conflict of interest.

Author details

Tamar Hopkins
University of Melbourne, Melbourne, Australia

*Address all correspondence to: tamar.blackwood@gmail.com

References

[1] Epp CR, Maynard-Moody S, Haider-Markel D. Pulled over: How Police Stops Define Race and Citizenship. Chicago: University of Chicago Press; 2014

[2] Alpert GP, Macdonald JM, Dunham RG. Police suspicion and discretionary decision making during citizen stops. Criminology. 2005;**43**(2):407-434

[3] Quinton P. The formation of suspicions: Police stop and search practices in England and Wales. Policing and Society. 2011;**21**(4):357-368

[4] Juanola MP. 'Unchecked' violence on the rise among Melbourne's rival street gangs. The Age. 2023. Available from: https://www.theage.com.au/national/victoria/viper-taskforce-to-strike-on-street-gangs-as-unchecked-violence-rises-20230207-p5cigg.html

[5] R v Buddee [2016] NSWDC 422

[6] Eddie R. Just 1 per cent of 'designated area' searches find illicit items. The Age. 13 Mar 2025. Available from: https://www.theage.com.au/politics/victoria/just-1-per-cent-of-designated-area-searches-find-illicit-items-20250313-p5ljdz.html

[7] Crutchfield RD, Skinner ML, Haggerty KP, McGlynn A, Catalano RF. Racial disparity in police contacts. Race and Justice. 2012;**2**(3):179-202

[8] Wiley SA, Esbensen FA. The effect of police contact: Does official intervention result in deviance amplification? Crime and Delinquency. 2016;**62**(3):283-307

[9] Ward JT, Krohn MD, Gibson CL. The effects of police contact on trajectories of violence. Journal of Interpersonal Violence. 2014;**29**(3):440-475

[10] Kane RJ. Compromised police legitimacy as a predictor of violent crime in structurally disadvantaged communities. Criminology. 2005;**43**(2):469-497

[11] Rios VM. The hyper-criminalization of black and Latino male youth in the era of mass incarceration. Souls: A Critical Journal of Black Politics, Culture, and Society. 2006;**8**(2):40-54

[12] Cunneen C. Conflict, Politics and Crime, Aboriginal Communities and the Police. Australia: Allen & Unwin; 2001

[13] Crime BH. Aboriginality and the Decolonisation of Justice. 2nd ed. Sydney: The Federation Press; 2016

[14] Fitzgerald R, Carrington P. Disproportionate minority contact in Canada: Police and visible minority youth. Canadian Journal of Criminology and Criminal Justice. 2011;**53**(4):449-486

[15] Meares T. Policing and procedural justice: Shaping citizens' identities to increase democratic participation. Northwestern University Law Review. 2017;**111**:1525-1536

[16] Tyler TR, Goff PA, MacCoun RJ. The impact of psychological science on policing in the United States: Proceedural justice, legitimacy, and effective law enforcement. Psychological Science in the Public Interest. 2015;**16**:75-109

[17] Futterman C, Hunt C, Kalven J. Youth/police encounters on Chicago's south side: Acknowledging the realities. The University of Chicago Legal Forum. 2016;**2016**:125-211, Article 5. Available

from: https://chicagounbound.uchicago.edu/uclf/vol2016/iss1/5/

[18] Butler P. Chokehold [Policing Black Men]. New York: The New Press; 2017

[19] Aranda E, Vaquera E. Unwelcomed immigrants: Experiences with immigration officials and attachment to the United States. Journal of Contemporary Criminal Justice. 2011;**27**(3):299-321

[20] Weber L. You're Going to be in the System Forever: Policing, Risk and Belonging in Greater Dandenong. Melbourne: Monash University; 2020 Apr

[21] Welsh Carroll M, Flanigan S, Gutierrez N III. Black lives experiencing homelessness matter: A critical conceptual framework for understanding how policing drives system avoidance among vulnerable populations. Public Integrity. 2022;**24**:1-16

[22] Lerman AE, Weaver VM. Staying out of sight, concentrated policing and local political action. Annals of the American Academy. 2015;**651**(651):202

[23] Ben-Menachem J, Morris KT. Ticketing and turnout: The participatory consequences of low-level police contact. American Political Science Review (Cambridge University Press). Aug 2023;**117**(3):822-834

[24] LaHee D. Youth perspective: Stop and frisk: Racial profiling in contemporary urban America. Children's Legal Rights Journal. 2016;**36**(1):8-23

[25] Poynting S. When zero tolerance looks like racial intolerance: 'Lebanese youth gangs', discrimination and resistance. Current Issues in Criminal Justice. 1999;**11**(1):74-78

[26] Hopkins T. Understanding Racial Profiling in Australia [PhD]. Sydney: UNSW; 2022

[27] Hopkins T, Popovic G. Do Australian police engage in racial profiling? A method for identifying racial profiling in the absence of police data. Current Issues in Criminal Justice. 2025;**37**(1):19-40

[28] Barkworth JM, Murphy K. Procedural justice policing and citizen compliance behaviour: The importance of emotion. Psychology, Crime and Law. 2015;**21**(3):254-273

[29] Sakkal P. 2019 Illicit Drugs Found in One in Four Cars Inspected Heading to Music Festival. The Age. Available from: https://www.theage.com.au/national/victoria/illicit-drugs-found-in-one-in-four-cars-inspected-heading-to-music-festival-20191209-p53i1d.html

[30] Oliveira A, Murphy K. Race, social identity, and perceptions of police bias. Race and Justice. 2015;**5**(3):259-277

[31] Bayley DH. What do the police do? In: Newburn T, editor. Policing, Key Readings. London: Routledge; 2005

[32] Ericson RV. The police as reproducers of order. In: Newburn T, editor. Policing, Key Readings. London: Routledge; 2005

[33] Skolnick JH, Fyfe JJ. Above the Law, Police and the Excessive Use of Force. New York: The Free Press; 1993

[34] Blagg H, Morgan N, Cunneen C, Ferrante A. Systemic racism as a factor in the over-representation of aboriginal people in the Victorian criminal justice system. Victorian Equal Opportunity and Human Rights Commission. 2005

Chapter 8

The State, the Police and Instability in Guinea: Reflections on Institutions of Security in a West African State

Ibrahim Bangura

Abstract

The relationship between the state, security institutions, and political instability in Guinea is deeply intertwined with the country's colonial legacy, governance structures, and socio-political dynamics. As a former French colony that gained independence in 1958, Guinea has experienced authoritarian rule, military interventions, and contested democratic transitions, all of which have influenced its security apparatus. The police, as a key institution of internal security, have often been implicated in human rights abuses, political repression, and corruption, raising concerns about their legitimacy and effectiveness. This chapter seeks to analyse the role of the state and police in managing stability and insecurity in Guinea, while reflecting on broader institutional reforms needed to enhance security governance.

Keywords: the state, police, security, stability, institutions

1. Introduction

The nexus between the state, the police, and societal (in)stability in Guinea reveals a complex and paradoxical dynamic. Since independence, Guinea has been shaped by a legacy of authoritarian rule, in which the security sector—comprising the military, police, and other coercive arms of the state—has functioned not as a neutral arbiter of law and order, but rather as a politicised and often repressive apparatus serving the regime's interests [1–3]. Repeated episodes of police brutality, impunity, and militarised responses to dissent have deepened public distrust and resentment, perpetuating cycles of instability and weakening democratic governance.

Guinea's postcolonial trajectory mirrors many of the challenges faced across the region: chronic political instability, ethnic polarisation, weak institutional capacity, endemic corruption, and the mismanagement of abundant natural resources. Despite its vast mineral wealth, the country remains one of the world's poorest, ranking 181st on the Human Development Index as of 2022 [4]. Within this context, the security sector has become increasingly politicised, shaped by internal rivalries and regularly embroiled in elite power struggles. Public perception of the security forces remains overwhelmingly negative, exacerbated by the judiciary's perceived ineffectiveness and political manipulation [3, 5].

Nonetheless, Guinea's recent political history has also been marked by pockets of resistance and calls for democratic reform, driven in large part by a vibrant civil society—including youth movements and trade unions—that has repeatedly challenged authoritarian overreach and demanded greater accountability [6, 7]. These democratic aspirations clashed dramatically with the events of 5 September 2021, when President Alpha Condé was ousted in a military coup led by Colonel Mamady Doumbouya. Condé's bid for a constitutionally dubious third term—secured through a controversial constitutional revision and disputed elections—provided the military with the pretext to seize power, promising a swift return to civilian rule. Yet, as of April 2025, this promised transition remains unfulfilled [8].

The enduring influence of the military, police and broader security sector in Guinea's political life underscores the urgent need for security sector reform grounded in democratic principles. Central to this is the establishment of effective civilian oversight mechanisms, the depoliticisation of law enforcement, and the development of institutions that can ensure transparency, accountability, and respect for human rights. Achieving such reform, however, depends not only on domestic political will but also on the sustained engagement of regional and international actors—including the African Union (AU), ECOWAS, the United States, France, and Guinea's neighbours. Yet the region's recent trend toward military rule and the international community's tepid response have cast doubt on the prospects for meaningful transformation. Whether Guinea can break this cycle and establish a sustainable framework for democratic security governance remains an open and pressing question. However, Guinea stands out in West Africa for its resilience in the face of these destabilising trends. Despite experiencing multiple coups, entrenched authoritarianism, regional geopolitical volatility, and fraught civil-military relations, the country has avoided descending into full-scale civil conflict—a fate that has afflicted several of its neighbours [1–3]. This chapter explores the apparent paradox of Guinea's relative internal stability amid systemic dysfunction, focusing on the evolution of its security sector as both a source of repression and a stabilising political actor. By analysing the sector's role in sustaining state authority—often at the expense of civil liberties—the chapter aims to shed light on the country's broader security governance landscape.

To that end, this study explores the following questions: What roles have the police and wider security institutions played in shaping political (in)stability in Guinea? How have legacies of authoritarianism, military intervention, and politicised policing contributed to or mitigated against state fragility? Why has Guinea, despite deep structural weaknesses and recurring military coups, not experienced a total state collapse or civil war? And crucially, what are the prospects for democratic security sector reform in a context where both domestic power dynamics and international engagement appear increasingly ambivalent? These questions guide the chapter's critical reflection on the functions, failures, and future of Guinea's security institutions.

Theoretically, the chapter draws from scholarship on state fragility and security sector governance in postcolonial African states. It engages with frameworks of securitisation to understand how state actors justify the expansion of coercive power under the guise of maintaining public order, often at the expense of democratic rights. Additionally, the analysis considers how neo-patrimonialism and elite bargaining shape the internal configuration of security institutions and their loyalty to ruling regimes. The chapter further dialogues with studies on authoritarian resilience and the role of security forces as both instruments of regime survival and agents of political change, particularly in contexts where formal democratic transitions remain incomplete or cyclical.

Methodologically, this study adopts a qualitative, interpretive approach, combining secondary literature, policy reports, and press sources with primary material from expert interviews and field reports where available. Interviews were done with 42 (27 males and 15 females) people between January 2024 and March 2025. Those interviewed included former and currently serving security officials, civil society leaders, academics and ordinary Guineans. The data collection process was supported by two research assistants (one male and one female), with the study focused on Conakry, the capital city of Guinea.

The study situates Guinea's trajectory within regional and comparative African perspectives, offering both an empirical case study and broader reflections on the limits and possibilities of reforming security institutions in contexts of contested governance and historical distrust. While Guinea is the focus, the chapter contributes to wider debates on policing, legitimacy, and authoritarian governance in sub-Saharan Africa.

2. Security sector reform in fragile African states: Examination of theory and practice

Security Sector Reform (SSR) has become a cornerstone of international engagement in post-conflict and fragile African states. It is widely framed as a strategy to professionalise, depoliticise, and democratise security institutions in contexts where these institutions have historically been sources of instability, repression, and exclusion. In theory, SSR should foster security institutions that operate under civilian control, uphold the rule of law, and are accountable to citizens. However, in practice, the implementation of SSR in fragile African states often falls short of these aspirations. The persistence of state fragility, elite resistance, and donor-driven programming has contributed to a significant gap between SSR theory and practice. Bridging this gap requires rethinking SSR as a deeply political, context-sensitive process anchored in local legitimacy and long-term governance transformation.

At its conceptual core, SSR promotes the development of accountable, efficient, and inclusive security and justice institutions. It is meant to be holistic—targeting the police, armed forces, intelligence services, judiciary, and oversight mechanisms—and based on democratic principles such as transparency, rule of law, and human rights [9]. However, as recent research has shown, these normative frameworks are often poorly adapted to the realities of fragile states, where institutional weakness, political instability, and hybrid forms of authority dominate the security landscape [10]. In such settings, SSR cannot be treated as a technocratic exercise of institutional reconfiguration but must be understood as a political process that engages with power dynamics, informal governance, and citizen-state relations.

One of the key weaknesses in SSR implementation in Africa has been the overreliance on externally driven models that fail to gain local traction. International actors—ranging from the UN and EU to bilateral donors like the United Kingdom, the United States, and France—often introduce SSR templates that reflect liberal peacebuilding norms but do not adequately account for national political economies or historical grievances. For instance, in Mali, extensive SSR programming since the 2013 international intervention has focused on restructuring the army and police, yet it failed to prevent the collapse of civilian control and the recurrence of military coups in 2020 and 2021 [11]. The emphasis on building capacity without addressing elite incentives or public legitimacy has contributed to what scholars' call "SSR without transformation" [12].

Similarly, in the Central African Republic (CAR), SSR has been integrated into broader peacekeeping and state-building efforts. Yet, the government remains heavily reliant on foreign military actors (notably Russia and France), and local SSR initiatives have struggled to demobilise armed groups or rebuild trust in national institutions [13]. These failures highlight the absence of meaningful local ownership, a principle routinely cited but rarely fulfilled. As Chappuis and Gorur [14] argue, true local ownership is not about involving elites in donor workshops but about shifting decision-making power to domestic actors and embedding reform in the political and social fabric of the country.

Another factor widening the theory-practice gap is the limited engagement with non-state and hybrid security providers. In fragile African states, the state is not the sole—or even primary—provider of security. Traditional leaders, vigilante groups, community self-defence forces, and private actors play key roles in everyday security governance. Yet SSR initiatives have often ignored or marginalised these actors. In Nigeria's northeast, for example, the Civilian Joint Task Force (CJTF) has been instrumental in resisting Boko Haram but remains outside formal oversight mechanisms and has been accused of human rights violations [15]. Integrating such actors into SSR requires new thinking about hybrid governance and the role of informal institutions in post-conflict reconstruction [16].

Moreover, SSR has often been approached in isolation from broader governance and development strategies. In fragile contexts, security provision is inseparable from questions of justice, inclusion, and service delivery. Rebuilding security institutions without parallel investments in judicial reform, anti-corruption mechanisms, and basic social services risks reinforcing authoritarian structures. In South Sudan, for instance, SSR has been repeatedly undermined by political elites using security institutions to entrench patronage and violently suppress dissent, even after the signing of peace agreements [17]. Sustainable SSR must therefore be nested within inclusive political settlements and wider public sector reform, not implemented as a stand-alone technical process.

Efforts to build trust between security institutions and citizens also remain underdeveloped. Public perceptions of security forces in fragile African states are often shaped by experiences of abuse, impunity, and neglect. Surveys by Afrobarometer [18] show that in countries like Guinea, Burkina Faso, and the DRC, most citizens distrust the police and see them as corrupt or abusive. SSR must prioritise community-oriented policing, mechanisms for complaint and redress, and inclusive consultation with women, youth, and marginalised communities. Experiences from Sierra Leone and Ghana demonstrate that when reforms are co-produced with civil society and accompanied by accountability tools, public confidence in security institutions can gradually be restored [19].

Sequencing and prioritisation also matter. The holistic vision of SSR may be appealing, but in fragile contexts with limited institutional capacity and resources, trying to reform all parts of the security sector at once is unrealistic. A more strategic approach involves identifying "entry points" for reform—such as creating internal disciplinary systems, establishing independent oversight bodies, or improving conditions of service for police officers—that can generate early wins and lay the groundwork for deeper change. Crucially, SSR must avoid over-securitisation and the militarisation of internal policing, which often alienate communities and provoke cycles of violence [20].

To bridge the gap between theory and practice, several policy shifts are essential. First, international partners must transition from project-based assistance to long-term partnerships, supporting iterative and adaptive processes rooted in local political realities. Second, SSR must be embedded in national political agendas, not treated as a donor-driven add-on. Third, local actors—including civil society, traditional authorities, and community security providers—must be empowered to shape the reform process. Fourth, accountability and human rights must be prioritised, not deferred in the name of stability. Finally, monitoring and evaluation systems should go beyond output metrics (e.g., number of personnel trained) and assess SSR's actual impact on security provision, citizen trust, and institutional behaviour.

In conclusion, while SSR remains a critical tool for rebuilding the state and strengthening public security in fragile African contexts, its transformative potential is undermined by a persistent disjuncture between its theoretical ambitions and practical outcomes. Closing this gap requires a fundamental recalibration—treating SSR not as a technical reform but as a political, participatory, and context-sensitive process. Only by grounding SSR in the lived realities of fragile states and prioritising legitimacy, inclusion, and accountability can reform truly contribute to peace and sustainable governance across Africa.

3. Historical context of law enforcement institutions in Guinea

Unlike many postcolonial African countries whose security architectures were deeply shaped by their former imperial rulers, Guinea's trajectory was markedly different. Upon declaring independence from France in 1958, Guinea experienced an abrupt and punitive withdrawal by the French, who destroyed administrative and military infrastructure, including weapons, buildings, archives, and key institutional assets that could have laid the foundation for an effective national security framework [21, 22]. The country was left without trained personnel or equipment and quickly turned toward the Eastern bloc—namely the Soviet Union and Cuba—as well as regional allies such as Ghana and Liberia for support. In this context, Guinea's post-independence security institutions emerged not from continuity or training by colonial administrators, but from a revolutionary vision tied to President Ahmed Sékou Touré's brand of African Socialism and party supremacy.

Initially envisioned as a "revolutionary army" independent of class or ethnic allegiance, the Guinean military was meant to defend the sovereignty of the nation, not to dominate it [21, 22]. However, this ideal was swiftly undermined by Touré's consolidation of authoritarian rule. The military, though powerful, was subordinated to a political logic of personal loyalty. Career advancement among senior officers was tied less to merit or professionalism and more to allegiance to Touré and the ruling party, with ethnic favouritism—particularly toward the Malinké group—serving as a key mechanism of political control [1, 3].

Paradoxically, while the military projected strength externally, the police were the true enforcers of state authority under Touré. Trained in Eastern bloc countries in surveillance and internal control, the Guinean police formed the backbone of an extensive domestic intelligence system. The country operated as a police state, with multiple layers of security embedded to prevent infiltration and monitor dissent. Touré's rule survived multiple attempted coups, and a 1970 Portuguese invasion attempt in large part due to the effectiveness of this internal apparatus, which also included militias and a Presidential Guard [21].

When Lansana Conté came to power following Touré's death in 1984, Guinea's security sector underwent significant transformation—though not necessarily toward democratic governance. The military regime under Conté expanded the size of the army substantially, from a few thousand under Touré to over 40,000 in the 1990s, particularly during periods of regional instability. However, this expansion was accompanied by widespread corruption and patrimonialism. High-ranking officers were rewarded with lucrative stakes in the privatised mining sector, while rank-and-file soldiers were poorly paid, neglected, and often deployed to deadly frontlines in Liberia, Sierra Leone, and Guinea-Bissau. Despite an increased defence budget—12.1% in 2007—the disparity between elites and ordinary soldiers bred resentment, culminating in frequent mutinies, coup attempts, and even hostage situations involving President Conté himself [1, 23].

Under Conté, Guinea saw formal moves toward democratisation, including the adoption of a new constitution in 1991 and the holding of multiparty elections in the 1990s and 2000s. However, these elections were marred by manipulation, and the underlying security and justice institutions remained unreformed. As protests intensified, driven by both civil society and security personnel themselves, the inability of the state to guarantee basic services or citizen protection became increasingly evident. In 2007, violent confrontations erupted not only between state forces and civilians but among security forces themselves. Military and police units clashed over salaries and conditions, and the army opened fire on civilians and fellow officers alike. These events reflected the deep institutional breakdown of Guinea's security sector, which had become a source of instability rather than a guarantor of it [3, 21].

The clearest manifestation of this dysfunction occurred on 28 September 2009, under the rule of Captain Moussa Dadis Camara, who had seized power in a coup following Conté's death in 2008. Despite initial promises to return Guinea to civilian rule, Camara declared his intention to run in the upcoming elections, prompting mass protests. During a peaceful demonstration at a stadium in Conakry, security forces massacred nearly 160 civilians, injured over 1200, and raped at least 100 women. This atrocity shocked the international community and underscored the extreme fragility, impunity, and politicisation of Guinea's security institutions. The massacre was not an isolated failure but the culmination of decades of authoritarian manipulation, ethnic favouritism, lack of professional oversight, and the absence of meaningful reform [3].

International pressure following the massacre—including sanctions, arms embargoes, and threats of prosecution by the International Criminal Court—contributed to Camara's fall from power. With his attempted assassination in late 2009 and the appointment of a transitional government, Guinea held its first relatively free presidential elections in 2010. Alpha Condé, a long-time opposition figure, was elected, raising hopes for a new era of democratic governance and genuine security sector reform.

However, Condé's presidency soon mirrored many of his predecessors in authoritarian style and disregard for democratic norms. While initial efforts were made in 2011–2012 to launch security sector reform initiatives—with international technical and financial support—these proved shallow in the absence of political will and institutional accountability. Condé's regime increasingly relied on repression, banning protests, targeting journalists, and using the security services to harass and torture political opponents. Despite its veneer of constitutionalism, his government retained many of the coercive hallmarks of Guinea's past regimes.

Crucially, this period reaffirmed that security sector reform (SSR) cannot succeed without robust security sector governance (SSG). Reform must go beyond restructuring or retraining; it requires democratic institutions that demand accountability, protect rights, and exert meaningful civilian oversight. The failure to establish such systems under Condé laid the groundwork for yet another military coup. In 2021, following a constitutional revision to allow for a third presidential term and a disputed electoral process, Condé was overthrown in a coup led by Colonel Mamady Doumbouya.

Guinea's long arc of authoritarianism—anchored in the manipulation of security forces—reveals that its greatest threats to peace and stability have often come not from insurgencies, regional spillovers, or religious extremism, but from the very institutions entrusted with maintaining order. The country's experience is a cautionary tale of how the militarisation of politics and the politicisation of the military can entrench a cycle of instability. Without a genuine commitment to democratic accountability, inclusive governance, and citizen-centred reform, Guinea's security sector will remain a powerful yet volatile actor—one more likely to threaten than to safeguard the republic.

4. The role of the police in Guinea's security architecture

The Guinean police force—comprising both the Police Nationale and the Gendarmerie—falls under the jurisdiction of the Ministry of Security and Civil Protection. Its official mandate includes maintaining public order, enforcing legal frameworks, and safeguarding citizen rights. Nevertheless, its operational capacity has been undermined by structural weaknesses, chronic underfunding, political interference, and an entrenched culture of impunity. Inter-agency rivalry and the absence of effective coordination mechanisms among the various branches of law enforcement further diminish institutional coherence and operational efficiency.[1]

Historically, the police have served as instruments of political repression, particularly under authoritarian regimes. Numerous human rights reports have documented patterns of arbitrary arrest, torture, and extrajudicial killings, especially targeting opposition groups and civil society actors [7, 24–26]. In addition to these abuses, endemic corruption, insufficient professional training, and inadequate remuneration have constrained the force's ability to fulfil its core public security functions.

The security services have rarely functioned as impartial guardians of the public good. Rather, they have frequently acted as coercive instruments of state power. This is particularly evident in the state's violent responses to popular protest, often triggered by deteriorating socio-economic conditions. As noted by 32 out of the 47 interviewees, the police react as directed by political elites. This they say has become much more precarious currently as there is a military regime in place, and the constitution is suspended. To the respondents, under various regimes, civilian and military, security forces have engaged in systematic repression of civic activism, thereby contributing to a climate of fear and political exclusion. A pervasive lack of internal discipline, widespread disregard for legal norms, and predatory behaviour toward civilians have characterised police conduct across successive administrations. These patterns have been facilitated—if not actively encouraged—by political elites who have consistently

[1] Based on interviews conducted for this study.

instrumentalised the police to entrench their rule, while failing to establish meaningful oversight or accountability structures.

This securitised approach to governance has contributed to the securitisation of dissent and the normalisation of police violence. The positioning of security forces as regime loyalists, rather than neutral state actors, has produced volatile dynamics within the security sector itself. Notably, the state's reliance on repression has not insulated it from internal threats, as evidenced by recurrent mutinies, coups d'état, and rebellions originating from within the armed forces.

Under the presidency of Alpha Condé, initial gains from limited security sector reform efforts were largely reversed. Following the 2018 ban on street protests, the Guinean police were implicated in the excessive use of force against demonstrators, resulting in over 100 deaths—approximately 40% of whom were minors [7, 24]. Respondents indicated during interviews that detainees have been held arbitrarily and subjected to protracted detention within a judicial system that is widely perceived as corrupt and politicised. Moreover, they argued that indiscriminate violence has extended to bystanders during protest events, further highlighting the lack of restraint and accountability within law enforcement structures.

Security forces have also been deployed to protect elite economic interests. For example, in 2021, the police reportedly used lethal force to suppress opposition to the operations of multinational mining companies, some of which maintain close ties with the ruling administration [7]. These instances illustrate the convergence of political repression and economic extraction, facilitated through coercive state apparatuses.

4.1 Public perceptions of law enforcement and legitimacy

Based on interviews and reviews done for this study, public confidence in law enforcement remains markedly low. Law enforcement institutions are widely perceived as corrupt, politically captured, and disconnected from the communities they ostensibly serve. The absence of robust accountability mechanisms has fostered a culture of impunity, further eroding public trust. While initiatives aimed at fostering community policing have been introduced, these have yielded limited success due to resource constraints and institutional resistance to reform.

Findings from the 2024 Afrobarometer survey underscore the depth of citizen disillusionment. Regarding the gendarmerie, which is a paramilitary wing of the Guinea police, 36.5% of respondents expressed no confidence whatsoever, while 23.9% reported low confidence and 21.4% partial confidence. Similarly, trust in the judiciary remains low: 26% of respondents indicated no confidence, 24.9% little confidence, and 20.7% partial confidence. Furthermore, 32.8% believed that the judiciary operates according to political influence rather than legal principles. These views are supported by respondents engaged during this study. Out of the 47 interviewees for this study, 42 indicated that they do not have confidence in the judiciary, as it is influenced and controlled by political elites. As stated by a civil society activist interviewed in Conakry:

> *The judiciary has never enjoyed the confidence of Guineans. When you have a case before them, find a political and not a legal solution. Those with better political connections get the outcome they desire. Here we have rule by law, not rule of law.*[2]

Similar sentiments were expressed by a former police officer:

[2] Interview conducted on 28 August 2024.

DOI: http://dx.doi.org/10.5772/intechopen.1010892

> *The judiciary has not been trained to function in the traditional sense of a judiciary. What they have is a pedestrian understanding of what they should be doing, and a deeper understanding of the need to satisfy the wishes of political elites. The Guinean state has been shaped since independence to embrace autocratic role, and no one wants to be seen challenging the existing system, and the judiciary falls within that bracket.*[3]

As observed by the respondent referenced above, what Guinea is contending with is a culture that has been entrenched since independence, and successive regimes have reinforced rather than seek to change it. Thus, that normalisation process has continuously undermined the potential for the practice of the rule of law, which has implications for the rights of those who seek justice and protection from the state.

According to the Afrobarometer survey [27], traditional and religious leaders enjoy considerably higher levels of public trust. The survey reported that 47.7% of respondents had high confidence in traditional leaders, and 64.3% in religious authorities, suggesting that these actors are perceived as more legitimate and accessible than formal state institutions. The reasons for this as argued by respondents that participated in interviews for this study, include factors such as trust in those institutions and how they function, and their willingness, accessibility and ability to engage and support the search for solutions to challenges in communities and households. Religious and traditional leaders provide significant social capital that people rely on, in the absence of law enforcement institutions they can trust.

The Afrobarometer survey [27] also reveals a profound disillusionment with democratic governance. A significant proportion of respondents—69.8%—exhibited indifference regarding the system of governance, reflecting the legacy of authoritarian rule, unfulfilled reform promises, and systemic violence against dissent. Only 13% expressed an unambiguous preference for democracy, while 16.4% supported alternative forms of governance under specific conditions. Attitudes toward civil society participation were ambivalent, with an even split between those affirming and rejecting the need for civil society involvement in governance. This sense of ambivalence and suspicion of democratic systems and institutions was attributed by respondents of this study, to the conducts of the Conté and Condé regimes that transitioned to democracy but used autocratic means to govern the state. They indicated that the election of Conde in 2010 as president inspired hope that was short lived, as he reneged on his promises and had to be eventually removed by the military in 2021.

5. Security sector governance and reform initiatives

With the ascendance of Condé to the presidency in 2010, he made attempts at undertaking security sector reform (SSR) and received substantial backing from international stakeholders. However, as noted by respondents, reform initiatives encountered significant impediments, notably resistance from entrenched political interests, limited financial resources, and inadequate training for security personnel. The enduring influence of patronage networks within the police and broader security apparatus continues to obstruct the development of professional and accountable institutions.

[3] Interview conducted in Conakry on 30 August 2024.

As stated by respondents who are former and currently serving police officers, at present, two principal obstacles confront police reform in Guinea: chronic underfunding of the security sector and a persistent lack of political interest to institutionalise SSR and transform it into sustained governance. The trajectory of Guinea's security sector has been marked by episodic and fragmented capacity-building efforts. These range from the Soviet and Cuban training provided during the Sékou Touré regime to the more Western-oriented approaches adopted in the later years of the Conté and Condé administrations [21–23]. Nevertheless, the periodic use of excessive force by security actors has resulted in international condemnation and sanctions, which in turn have disrupted external support and impeded long-term capacity-building initiatives.

Support from Western actors and regional organisations such as ECOWAS and the African Union remains largely conditional on the fulfilment of good governance benchmarks, including transparency and accountability—areas in which Guinea has consistently underperformed [28, 29]. Rebuilding efforts have been constrained by capital shortages and limited human resource capacity. Intra-agency rivalries, periodic purges, and the prioritisation of ethnic and regime loyalty over merit and training further undermine reform prospects. Collectively, these dynamics have impeded the emergence of a disciplined, professional, and trusted security sector.

Some of the support to SSR initiatives undertaken included the Partners for Security in Guinea: Police Reform Serving the Citizen (SINLEC) project, a five-year (2015–2020) project funded by the United States Department of State and implemented by COGINTA and CEDIDE. The project supported trust building between the citizens and the Guinean police.[4]

On a national scale, SSR initiatives initially focused on fostering accountability, inclusivity, public trust, and the prevention of future human rights abuses. In response to the 2009 stadium massacre, the United Nations advocated for the establishment of a Truth, Justice and Reconciliation Committee and a National Human Rights Commission [31]. The UN Peacebuilding Support Office in Guinea (UNOGBIS) sought to initiate dialogue between civil society and security actors and supported the development of a national peace infrastructure [3]. The National Strategy for Priority Actions, adopted in May 2014, aimed to consolidate these reform efforts [32]. However, as noted by respondents, the implementation of these measures has been severely hampered by a lack of political commitment, misallocation of budgetary resources, and weak institutional capacity. The Truth, Justice and Reconciliation Committee remains inactive, with the last recorded progress being the introduction of a bill in 2017. The National Human Rights Commission has yet to be established, and the mandate of the Peacebuilding Support Office is currently under review.

Captain Moussa Dadis Camara, the former Guinean military ruler implicated in the 2009 stadium massacre, was convicted in 2024 for crimes against humanity and sentenced to 20 years in prison. However, in a decision that shocked international observers and raised serious concerns about the trajectory of justice in Guinea, President Mamady Doumbouya granted him a presidential pardon in March 2025. This controversial move has cast a long shadow over the credibility of Guinea's judicial system and is widely viewed as a setback for accountability efforts. It highlights the

[4] See: Ref. [30].

enduring fragility of international SSR initiatives when domestic political calculations override commitments to human rights and the rule of law.[5]

It is worth noting that by 2020, the Guinean state was largely a police state, with SSR efforts being very minimal, as President Condé was focused on securing a third term and gendarmerie were deployed across the country to deal with opposition and those with dissenting views. As most of the respondents stated during interviews, this further deepened frustrations on the part of the public in the police and other law enforcement agencies, as initiatives that were focused on building trust between them.

Overall, while SSR in Guinea has achieved some isolated improvements—particularly at the local level—national-level reform continues to be undermined by entrenched political dynamics, institutional fragility, and the conditional nature of international support. The path toward comprehensive, sustainable reform remains complex and uncertain.

6. Policy reflection: Priority actions for reforming law enforcement institutions in Guinea

Respondents noted during interviews that there are immediate and urgent steps to be taken to address the gaps in the law enforcement agencies in Guinea. They indicated that improving Guinea's law enforcement institutions requires a coherent and sequenced set of actions grounded in principles of professionalism, accountability, and proximity to the population.

A total of 23 out of the 47 respondents stated that the reform process must begin with the establishment of a National Independent Police Oversight Authority with clear investigative and disciplinary powers. This body, composed of representatives from civil society, legal institutions, and retired professionals, should be mandated by law to receive complaints, conduct independent investigations, and publish regular reports. They further stated that when the country returns to democracy, the legislative level, parliamentary oversight of the security sector should be institutionalised, with dedicated committees given access to police budgets, operational plans, and annual performance audits.

Most of the respondents stated that a comprehensive SSR process is required to stabilise the Guinean state, and such processes should address structural weaknesses, and that the recruitment and training systems must be reformed to ensure transparency and meritocracy. This should include the introduction of competitive and decentralised recruitment mechanisms supervised by independent boards with civil society observers, based on criteria that prioritise education, aptitude, and moral standing. In parallel, the police training curricula must be thoroughly revised and standardised. Furthermore, new curricula should integrate human rights, gender sensitivity, community-based policing, de-escalation techniques, and basic legal principles. The establishment of a National Police Academy and regional training centres will help ensure consistent professional development across the country. These institutions should also promote joint training programmes with justice officials and human rights organisations to improve procedural knowledge and civic orientation.

5 See: France 24 [33].

Tied to the above, most of the respondents stated that future SSR processes should ensure that institutional mandates are clarified to reduce fragmentation and rivalry. As stated by a lecturer in the University of Conakry:

> *A comprehensive legal review is needed to redefine the respective roles of the police, gendarmerie, and military in internal security in Guinea. A clear legal framework should specify the boundaries of law enforcement jurisdiction and explicitly limit the role of the military in civilian policing functions. This must be reinforced by the creation of formal inter-agency coordination platforms at national and regional levels, which will facilitate information sharing, coordinated planning, and joint operational readiness, particularly in areas of public order and criminal investigations.*[6]

However, inter-agency cooperation requires significant political interest and determination to be developed and to succeed. Guinea will need a clear break from the past, with a share determination on the part of political actors to transition to democratic governance, with a human security-based approach adopted to enhance the safety, security and dignity of Guineans.

A key recommendation by the respondents is the need to have an SSR process that builds trust between the police and the citizens. However, they noted that building public trust requires the institutionalisation of community policing models. They further recommended that the creation of Community Police Councils in each commune or prefecture—comprising police representatives, local authorities, youth groups, women's associations, and civil society organisations—will provide a structured forum for regular dialogue, conflict prevention, and shared responsibility in public safety. In parallel, specially trained community liaison officers should be deployed in marginalised or high-tension neighbourhoods. These officers must be equipped with mediation skills, cultural knowledge, and communication tools to serve as bridges between the population and the institution.

Majority of the respondents stated that professional incentives must be introduced and aligned with a human resource management system that links career advancement to performance, training, and ethical behaviour. A performance appraisal system should be introduced that includes community feedback, complaint records, and peer evaluations. This must be reinforced by a functional and well-resourced internal disciplinary system, governed by a clear code of conduct, with regular internal audits and transparent sanctions for misconduct. These measures are crucial for breaking patterns of impunity and for incentivising good conduct.

Improving the material and operational capacity of police services is another pillar of reform that needs to be considered by the Guinean state and their development partners. It was observed during reviews and interviews that many stations in Guinea are under-equipped, structurally inadequate, and lack the basic tools for effective policing. A comprehensive investment programme in infrastructure and logistics is required, covering station rehabilitation, uniforms, vehicles, communication systems, and forensic tools. Alongside this, the digitalisation of administrative systems—including personnel records, case tracking, and internal complaint databases—will support transparency, efficiency, and oversight.

To ensure public legitimacy, police transparency and public engagement must be institutionalised. This includes the mandatory publication of annual reports

[6] Interview conducted virtually on 11 March 2025.

by the national police authority, detailing operations, crime trends, reform measures, and disciplinary outcomes. Public communication strategies must also be strengthened. A nationwide public awareness campaign on citizens' rights and police responsibilities should be launched using accessible formats—radio, social media, mobile messaging, and public events. This campaign should explain the reform agenda, encourage the use of grievance mechanisms, and support civic empowerment.

These reforms require political commitment, resource mobilisation, and long-term engagement. They must be implemented in an inclusive manner, with participation from civil society, local governments, professional associations, and international partners. While international support may be needed to provide technical assistance, training, and funding, the leadership and ownership of the reform must rest firmly with Guinean institutions. Only through such a multidimensional and context-sensitive strategy can Guinea build law enforcement institutions that are professional, accountable, and genuinely in the service of its citizens. To adopt these changes, the 2010 Constitution should be reviewed to enhance the rights and freedoms through strengthening laws and institutions that promote and protect them.

7. Conclusion

Guinea's security architecture reflects a troubling legacy of authoritarianism, politicisation, and violent repression, embedded within both its military and police institutions. Historically moulded as instruments of regime preservation rather than protectors of citizens, these security structures have become synonymous with human rights abuses, impunity, and institutional decay. Despite moments of attempted reform, particularly in the post-2009 era, political manipulation, ethnic favouritism, and a lack of sustained democratic governance have repeatedly undermined progress. The police and military, instead of ensuring public safety, have cyclically been perpetrators of violence—against civilians, opposition voices, and even among themselves—highlighting the urgent need for transformative reform rooted in accountability, civilian oversight, and institutional integrity.

This institutional dysfunction is mirrored in Guinea's volatile political transitions, where the oscillation between civilian and military regimes has stunted democratic consolidation. The current junta, led by Mamady Doumbouya, follows a pattern of broken promises and repression, despite overwhelming popular and international support for a return to constitutional rule. The erosion of public trust, as reflected in the Afrobarometer findings, speaks to a citizenry deeply disillusioned with governance structures that consistently fail to deliver justice, security, or representation.

Yet, within this grim landscape lies a resilient civil society—young, vocal, and determined to claim space in Guinea's political future. For sustainable peace and institutional renewal, Guinea must foster genuine dialogue between civil society, traditional leaders, and security actors, while embracing regional and international support mechanisms. Reform efforts must move beyond technical fixes to embrace holistic security sector governance that is democratic, inclusive, and accountable. Without such foundational change, Guinea risks perpetuating its cycle of instability, repression, and missed opportunities for transformation.

Author details

Ibrahim Bangura
Department of Peace and Conflict Studies, Fourah Bay College, University of Sierra Leone, Sierra Leone

*Address all correspondence to: bangural@yahoo.co.uk

References

[1] Clarke P. Guinea: The History of the Military as a Political Actor. Oxford Research Encyclopaedia of Politics. Oxford, United Kingdom: Oxford University Press; 2021. DOI: 10.1093/acrefore/9780190228637.013.1894

[2] Devermont J. Guinea: The Causes and Consequences of West Africa's Latest Coup [Online]. Centre for Strategic and International Studies. Washington, DC. USA.; 2021. Available from: https://www.csis.org/analysis/guinea-causes-and-consequences-west-africas-latest-coup [Accessed: April 8, 2025]

[3] Stefan CG. Lessons in atrocity prevention: A closer look at Guinea. Journal of International Peacekeeping. 2021;**24**(3-4):367-401. DOI: 10.1163/18754112-24030005

[4] UNDP. Human Development Index - Guinea [online]. New York: UNDP; 2022. Available from: https://hdr.undp.org/data-center/specific-country-data#/countries/GIN [Accessed: April 5, 2025]

[5] Bangura I. Confronting a brutal present Guinean youth and the struggle against constitutional breach. In: Bangura I, editor. Youth Led Social Movements and Peacebuilding in Africa. UK: Routledge; 2022

[6] Kaye JL. What Works in UN Resident Coordinator-Led Conflict Prevention: Lessons from the Field (Republic of Guinea 2009-17). New York, United States: United Nations University Centre for Policy Research; 2018

[7] Szabo T. Guinea Joint Stakeholder Report for the United Nations Universal Periodic Review: Civil and Political Rights and Gender-Based Violence. Minneapolis, USA: The Advocates for Human Rights; 2024

[8] Siegle J, Wahila H. Guinea: Despite Protests, Military Junta Angles to Perpetuate its Hold on Power [Online]. Africa Center for Strategic Studies. Washington D.C.; 2025. Available from: https://africacenter.org/spotlight/2025-elections/guinea/ [Accessed: April 4, 2025]

[9] OECD. Security System Reform and Governance: Policy Framework. Paris: OECD Publishing; 2020

[10] Idris I. SSR in Conflict-Affected and Fragile States. K4D Helpdesk Report. UK: FCDO; 2021

[11] Ba B, Cold-Ravnkilde SM. Mali's Interim Government: Between Strategic Partnerships and Internal Fragility. Copenhagen: Danish Institute for International Studies (DIIS); 2021

[12] Sedra M. Security Sector Reform and State Building. Routledge Studies in Conflict, Security and Development. London: Routledge; 2018

[13] Lemay-Hébert N, Utas M, N'Diaye B. Hybrid security governance in Africa: Beyond state-centric models. African Affairs. 2023;**122**(486):121-142

[14] Chappuis F, Gorur A. Rethinking SSR: From Liberal Templates to Local Realities. Geneva, Switzerland: Geneva Centre for Security Sector Governance (DCAF); 2022

[15] International Crisis Group. The Civilian Joint Task Force: Beyond the Frontlines in Nigeria's War against Boko Haram. Africa Report No. 297. Brussels, Belgium: International Crisis Group; 2021

[16] Meagher K, De Herdt T, Titeca K. Unravelling public authority: Paths of hybrid governance in Africa. IDS Bulletin. 2019;**50**(1):1-6

[17] Rolandsen ØH. Security sector reform in South Sudan: The political economy of peacebuilding. Journal of Eastern African Studies. 2021;**15**(4):561-580

[18] Afrobarometer. Public Attitudes toward the Police in Africa: Trust, Effectiveness, and Accountability. Accra, Ghana: Afrobarometer; 2022. Available from: www.afrobarometer.org

[19] Bryden A, Olonisakin F, editors. Security Sector Transformation in Africa. Münster: LIT Verlag; 2010

[20] Hendrickson D, Ball N. The Politics of Security Sector Reform in Fragile States: Why the Assumptions Matter. London: ODI Working Paper; 2023

[21] Bah MD. The military and politics in Guinea: An instrumental explanation of political stability. Armed Forces & Society [online]. 2015;**41**(1):69-95. DOI: 10.2307/48609199

[22] Camara MS. From military politization to militarization of power in Guinea - Conakry. Journal of Political & Military Sociology [online]. 2000;**28**(2):311-326. DOI: 10.2307/45292817

[23] Bangoura D. Guinea. In: Security Sector Governance in Francophone West Africa: Realities & Opportunities. Geneva, Switzerland: Geneva Center for the Democratic Control of Armed Forces; 2011

[24] Amnesty International. Guinée: Victims of Illegal Use of Force Await Treatment and Justice [Online]. Amnesty International. London, United Kingdom; 2024. Available from: https://www.amnesty.org/fr/latest/news/2024/05/guinee-les-victimes-dusage-illegal-de-la-force-en-attente-de-soins-et-de-justice/ [Accessed: April 7, 2025]

[25] Human Rights Watch. Guinea: Rights at Risk as Promised Transition Derails [Online]. Human Rights Watch. New York, USA; 2024a. Available from: https://www.hrw.org/news/2024/12/02/guinea-rights-risk-promised-transition-derails [Accessed: April 3, 2025]

[26] Human Rights Watch. World Report 2025: Rights Trends in Guinea [Online]. Human Rights Watch. New York, USA; 2024b. Available from: https://www.hrw.org/world-report/2025/country-chapters/guinea [Accessed: April 3, 2025]

[27] Afrobarometer. Résumé des résultats - Round 10 en Guinea, 2024. Accra, Ghana: Afrobarometer; 2024

[28] Albrecht P. Transforming internal security in Sierra Leone and Guinea: A political approach to SSR. DIIS Report. 2010;**2010**:18

[29] Bryden A, Scherrer V. Reforming Intelligence: Democratic Control of Security Sector Reform in Guinea. Geneva: Geneva Centre for the Democratic Control of Armed Forces (DCAF); 2012

[30] Coginta. Partenaires pour la sécurité en Guinée: La réforme de la police au service du citoyen (SINULEC); n.d. Available from: https://coginta.org/en/projets/partenaires-pour-la-securite-en-guinee-la-reforme-de-la-police-au-service-du-citoyen-sinlec/ [Accessed: April 13, 2025]

[31] Human Rights Watch. Bloody Monday: The September 28 Massacre and Rapes by Security Forces in Guinea. New York, USA: Human Rights Watch; 2009.

Available from: https://www.hrw.org/report/2009/12/17/bloody-monday/september-28-massacre-and-rapes-security-forces-guinea

[32] Barry A. Guinea Plans a Truth Commission [online]. 2017. Available from: https://www.justiceinfo.net/en/33017-guinea-plans-a-truth-commission.html [Accessed: April 7, 2025].

[33] France 24. Guinea's Junta Leader Pardons 2009 Massacre Figure Captain Dadis Camara. France 24. Paris, France; 2025. Available from: https://www.france24.com/en/africa/20250322-guinea-s-junta-leader-pardons-2009-massacre-figure-captain-dadis-camara [Accessed: April 13, 2025]